Okay-okay! I know you're eager to start training but first let me fill you in on

HOW TO USE THIS BOOK

This book is divided into three parts:

1. Writing practice sheets for 204 kanji symbols required for Japanese Language Proficiency Test Level N4 (JLPT N4)*

The fact of the matter is that you'll probably have to use up a lot of practice paper before you memorize Japanese kanji symbols. This workbook is designed in a way that you can cut pages out of it and copy them as much as you like in a copying machine. There's stroke order for each of kanji symbols as well as a few compound words that use those symbols.

2. Compound words writing practice

To become proficient in Japanese reading and writing it's not enough for you to learn individual kanji symbols. You also need to know how to read and write words that are composed from several kanji symbols i.e. compound words. And what is a better way to learn those words than writing them down several times? The second part of the book is devoted to this. There're over 250 words with JLPT N4 and N5 kanji symbols for you write.

3. Cut out flash cards for 103 kanji symbols for JLPT N4

Cut out these pages and then cut them again using cross marks. There you've got your own kanji flash cards with the symbol on one side and onyomi and kunyomi readings on another. No need to spend extra on buying those fancy cardboard cards!

Let me not hold you any further!

(Benkyō shiyou! - Let's study!)

* As of 2010, there is no official kanji list. The symbols that are listed in this workbook are an educated guess of what might come up in the N4 exam.

Please note that this book doesn't include kanji symbols needed for JLPT N5 exam. You can practice writing those symbols with our 3-in-1 JLPT N5 Workbook.

We are happy to accept corrections and feedback regarding this workbook at:
lilas.publishing@ya.ru

Lilas Lingvo

Hiragana letters chart

gojūon

	a-column	*i*-column	*u*-column	*e*-column	*o*-column
a-row	あ a	い i	う u	え e	お o
ka-row	か ka	き ki	く ku	け ke	こ ko
sa-row	さ sa	し shi	す su	せ se	そ so
ta-row	た ta	ち chi	つ tsu	て te	と to
na-row	な na	に ni	ぬ nu	ね ne	の no
ha-row	は ha	ひ hi	ふ fu	へ he	ほ ho
ma-row	ま ma	み mi	む mu	め me	も mo
ya-row	や ya	い i	ゆ yu	え e	よ yo
ra-row	ら ra	り ri	る ru	れ re	ろ ro
wa-row	わ wa	い i	う u	え e	を o
			ん n		

yōon

きゃ kya	きゅ kyu	きょ kyo
しゃ sha	しゅ shu	しょ sho
ちゃ cha	ちゅ chu	ちょ cho
にゃ nya	にゅ nyu	にょ nyo
ひゃ hya	ひゅ hyu	ひょ hyo
みゃ mya	みゅ myu	みょ myo
りゃ rya	りゅ ryu	りょ ryo

dakuon

	a-column	*i*-column	*u*-column	*e*-column	*o*-column
ga-row	が ga	ぎ gi	ぐ gu	げ ge	ご go
za-row	ざ za	じ ji	ず zu	ぜ ze	ぞ zo
da-row	だ da	ぢ ji	づ zu	で de	ど do
ba-row	ば ba	び bi	ぶ bu	べ be	ぼ bo

ぎゃ gya	ぎゅ gyu	ぎょ gyo
じゃ ja	じゅ ju	じょ jo
ぢゃ ja	ぢゅ ju	ぢょ jo
びゃ bya	びゅ byu	びょ byo

han-dakuon

	a-column	*i*-column	*u*-column	*e*-column	*o*-column
pa-row	ぱ pa	ぴ pi	ぷ pu	ぺ pe	ぽ po

ぴゃ pya	ぴゅ pyu	ぴょ pyo

additional letters for foreign sounds

ゔ　ぁ　ぃ　ぅ　ぇ　ぉ
e.g. ゔぃ (vi), ふぁ (fa), てぃ (ti), どぅ (du), うぇ (we), ふぉ (fo)

sokuon

っ
pause (no sound)

Katakana letters chart

gojūon

	a-column	*i*-column	*u*-column	*e*-column	*o*-column
a-row	ア a	イ i	ウ u	エ e	オ o
ka-row	カ ka	キ ki	ク ku	ケ ke	コ ko
sa-row	サ sa	シ shi	ス su	セ se	ソ so
ta-row	タ ta	チ chi	ツ tsu	テ te	ト to
na-row	ナ na	ニ ni	ヌ nu	ネ ne	ノ no
ha-row	ハ ha	ヒ hi	フ fu	ヘ he	ホ ho
ma-row	マ ma	ミ mi	ム mu	メ me	モ mo
ya-row	ヤ ya	イ i	ユ yu	エ e	ヨ yo
ra-row	ラ ra	リ ri	ル ru	レ re	ロ ro
wa-row	ワ wa	イ i	ウ u	エ e	ヲ o
	ン n				

dakuon

ga-row	ガ ga	ギ gi	グ gu	ゲ ge	ゴ go
za-row	ザ za	ジ ji	ズ zu	ゼ ze	ゾ zo
da-row	ダ da	ヂ ji	ヅ zu	デ de	ド do
ba-row	バ ba	ビ bi	ブ bu	ベ be	ボ bo

han-dakuon

pa-row	パ pa	ピ pi	プ pu	ペ pe	ポ po

additional letters for foreign sounds

ヴ	ア	イ	ウ	エ	オ

e.g. ヴィ (vi), ファ (fa), ティ (ti), ドゥ (du), ウェ (we), フォ (fo)

yōon

キャ kya	キュ kyu	キョ kyo
シャ sha	シュ shu	ショ sho
チャ cha	チュ chu	チョ cho
ニャ nya	ニュ nyu	ニョ nyo
ヒャ hya	ヒュ hyu	ヒョ hyo
ミャ mya	ミュ myu	ミョ myo
リャ rya	リュ ryu	リョ ryo
ギャ gya	ギュ gyu	ギョ gyo
ジャ ja	ジュ ju	ジョ jo
ヂャ ja	ヂュ ju	ヂョ jo
ビャ bya	ビュ byu	ビョ byo
ピャ pya	ピュ pyu	ピョ pyo

sokuon

ツ
pause (no sound)

Contents

不

non-; negative; bad

onyomi フ、ブ
kunyomi
compounds 不便（ふべん）inconvenience

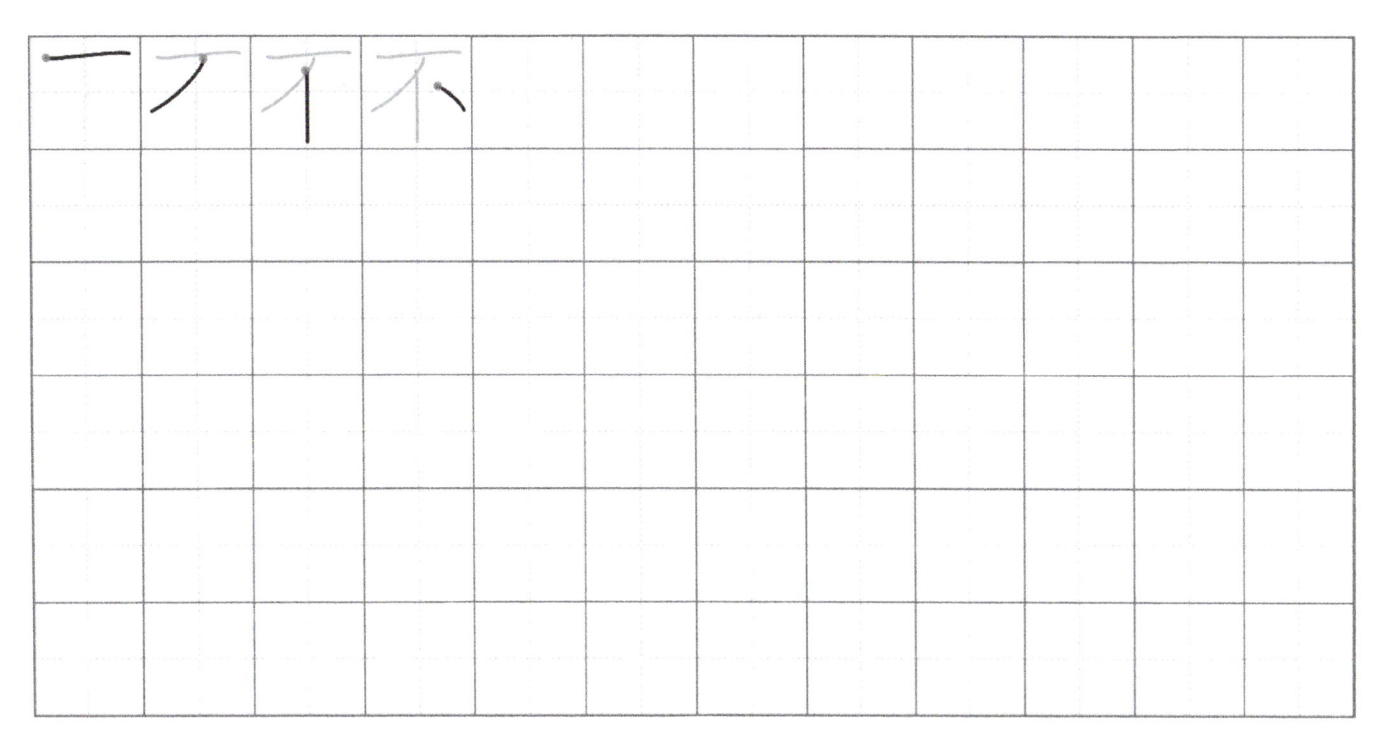

世

generation; public; society; world

onyomi セ、セイ、ソウ
kunyomi よ
compounds 世界（せかい）world
世話（せわ）looking after

主

chief; lord; main thing; master; principal

onyomi	シュ、シュウ、ス
kunyomi	おも、ぬし
compounds	ご主人 (ごしゅじん) (hon) your husband

honorific

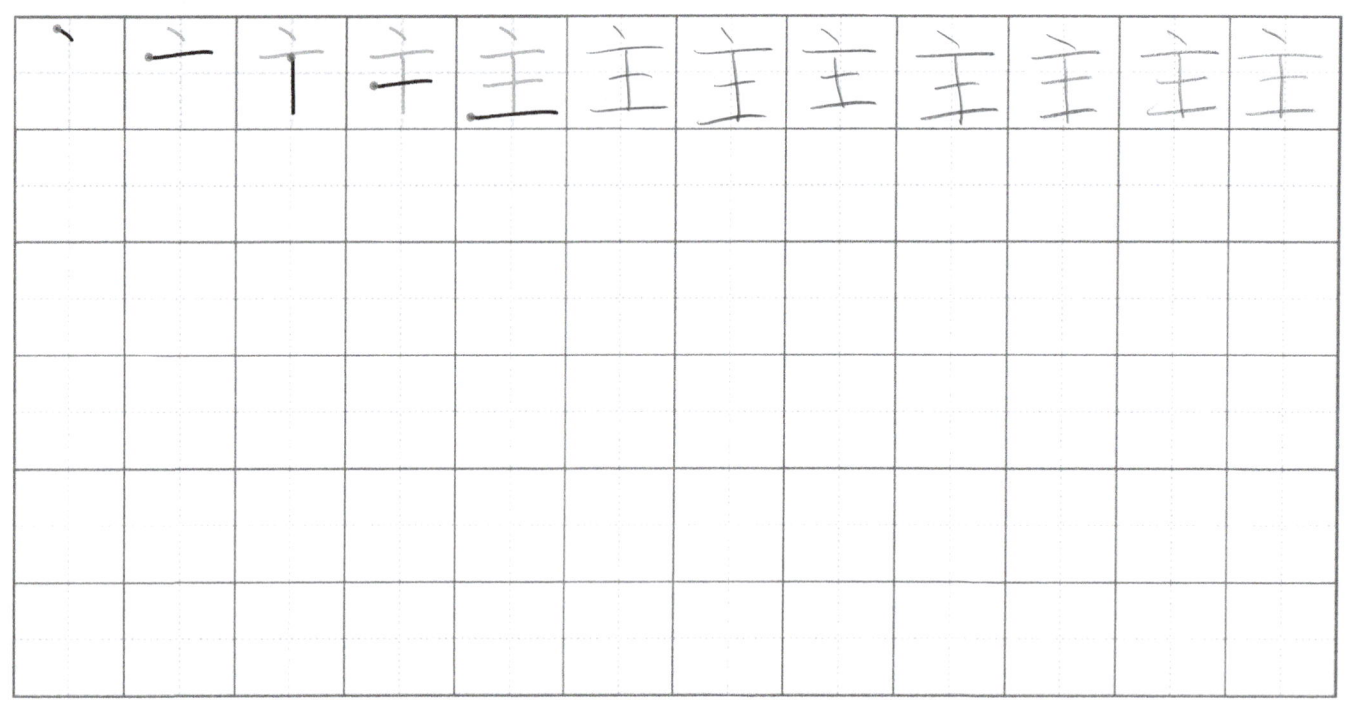

乗

board; ride; counter for vehicles; multiplication; power

onyomi	ショウ、ジョウ　(に のります)
kunyomi	の・せる、の・る
compounds	乗り換える (のりかえる) to transfer/change (bus, train)
	乗り物 (のりもの) vehicle
	乗る (のる) to get on (train, plane, bus, ship, etc.); to ride; to board

事

business; fact; matter; possibly; reason; thing

onyomi	ジ
kunyomi	こと
compounds	事務所 (じむしょ) office
	事故 (じこ) accident; incident; trouble
	仕事 (しごと) work; job; business
	返事 (へんじ) reply; response

京

capital

onyomi	キョウ
kunyomi	みやこ
compounds	京都 (きょうと) Kyoto

attend; doing; official; serve

onyomi	シ、ジ
kunyomi	つか・える
compounds	仕事 (しごと) work; job; business
	仕方 (しかた) way; method; means

change; replace; substitute; convert; counter for decades of ages; fee; generation; period

onyomi	タイ、ダイ
kunyomi	かわ・る、か・える
compounds	代わり (かわり) substitute; replacement
	時代 (じだい) period; era; times

仕、代

以

because; by means of; compared with

onyomi	イ
kunyomi	
compounds	以上 (いじょう) more than (or equal to); at least
	以下 (いか) less than (or equal to); below
	以内 (いない) within; up to; less than
	以外 (いがい) with the exception of; other than

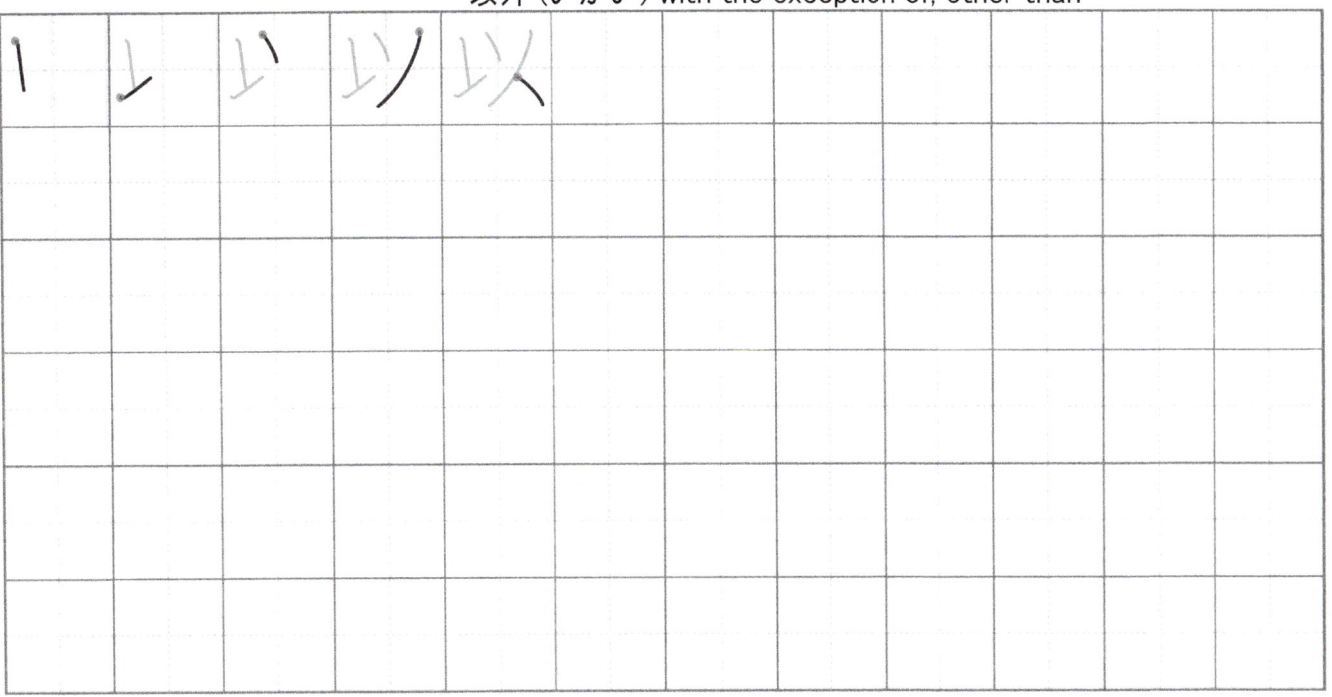

会

association; interview; join; meet; meeting; party

onyomi	エ、カイ
kunyomi	あ・う、あ・わせる、あつ・まる
compounds	会う (あう) to meet
	会場 (かいじょう) assembly hall; venue
	会社 (かいしゃ) company
	会議 (かいぎ) meeting; conference

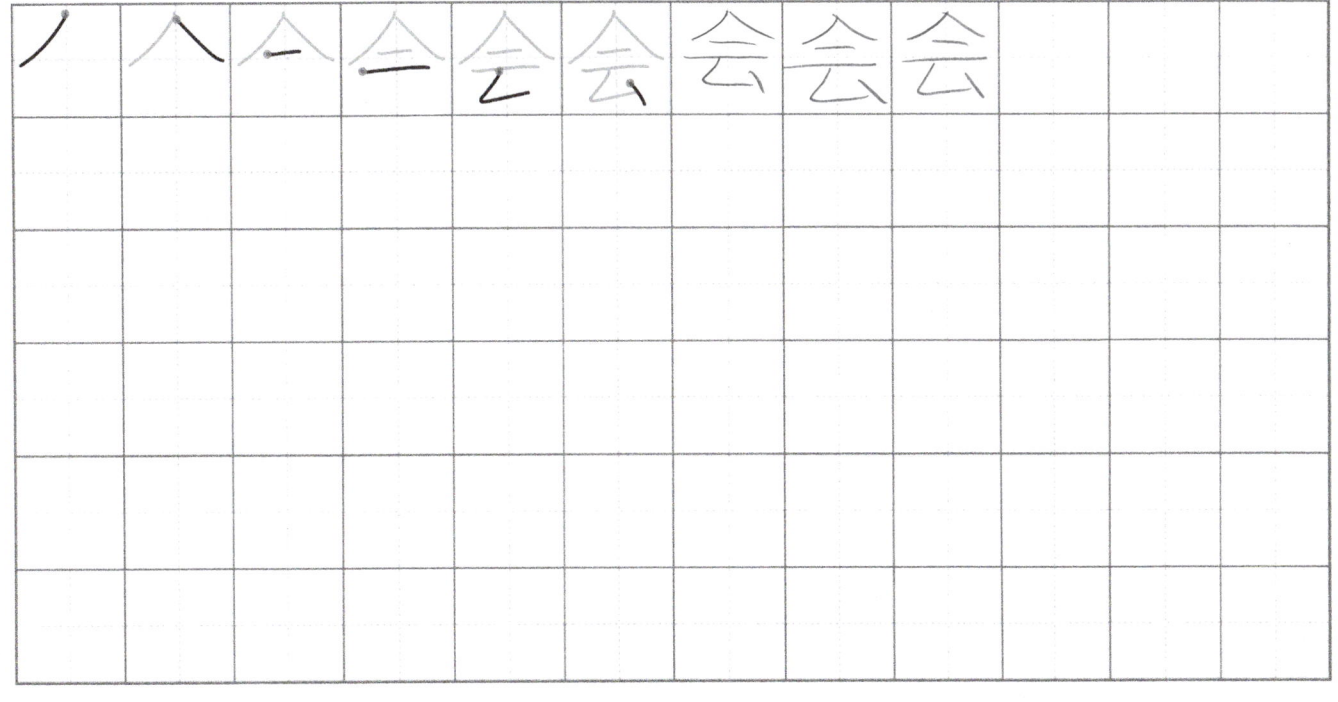

低

humble; lower; short

onyomi	テイ
kunyomi	ひく・い、ひく・まる、ひく・める
compounds	低い (ひくい) low (rank, volumn, etc.) | short (height); low (position)

住

live; reside

（にすんでいます）

onyomi	ジュウ、チュウ、ヂュウ
kunyomi	す・まう、す・む
compounds	住む (すむ) to live; to reside; to inhabit
	住所 (じゅうしょ) address (e.g. of house)

低、住

体

body; object; substance

onyomi	タイ、テイ
kunyomi	かたち、からだ
compounds	体（からだ）body
	大体（だいたい）generally; approximately

作

build; make; prepare; production

onyomi	サ、サク
kunyomi	つく・り、つく・る
compounds	作る（つくる）to make; to produce; to manufacture
	作文（さくぶん）writing; composition

使

ambassador; use

onyomi	シ
kunyomi	つか・い、つか・う
compounds	使う（つかう）to use
	大使館（たいしかん）embassy

ノ　イ　仁　仁　仁　信　伊　使　使　使　使　使

便

convenience; facility; feces; letter

onyomi	ビン、ベン
kunyomi	たよ・り
compounds	不便（ふべん）inconvenience
	便利（べんり）convenient; handy; useful
	郵便局（ゆうびんきょく）post office

ノ　イ　仁　仁　信　信　信　便　便

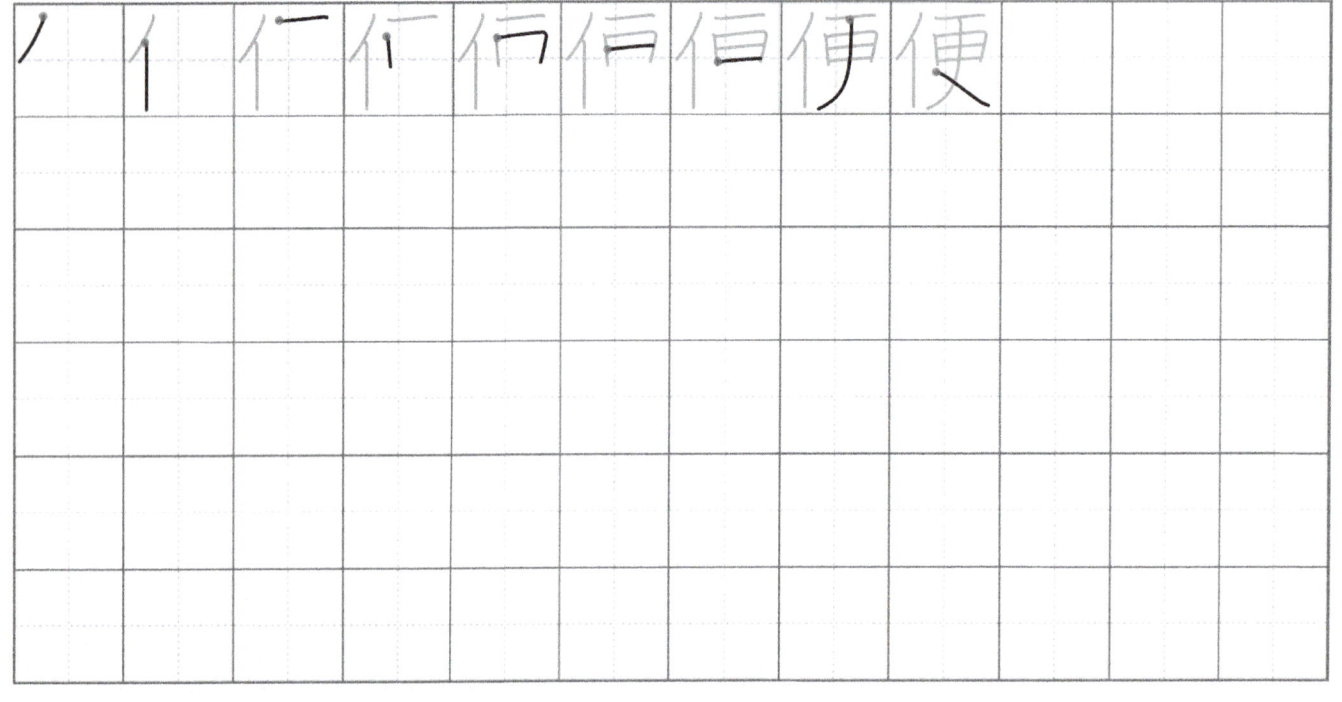

借

onyomi　シャク
kunyomi　か・りる
compounds　借りる (かりる) to borrow; to have a loan | to rent

働

work

onyomi　ドウ
kunyomi　はたら・く
compounds　働く (はたらく) to work; to labor

元

beginning; origin; former time

onyomi	ガン、ゲン
kunyomi	もと
compounds	元気 (げんき) healthy; well; lively

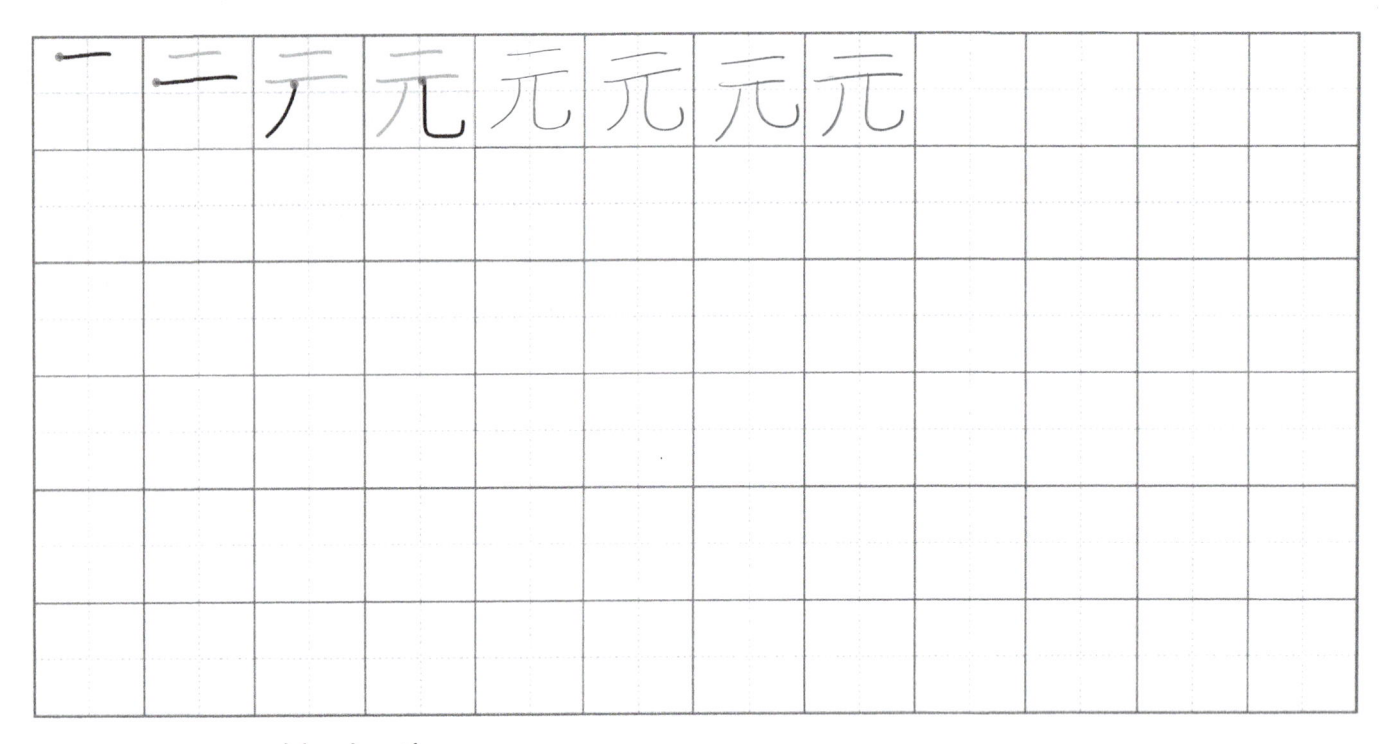

兄

elder brother

onyomi	キョウ
kunyomi	あに
compounds	お兄さん (おにいさん) older brother
	兄 (あに) (hum) older brother
	兄弟 (きょうだい) siblings; brothers and sisters

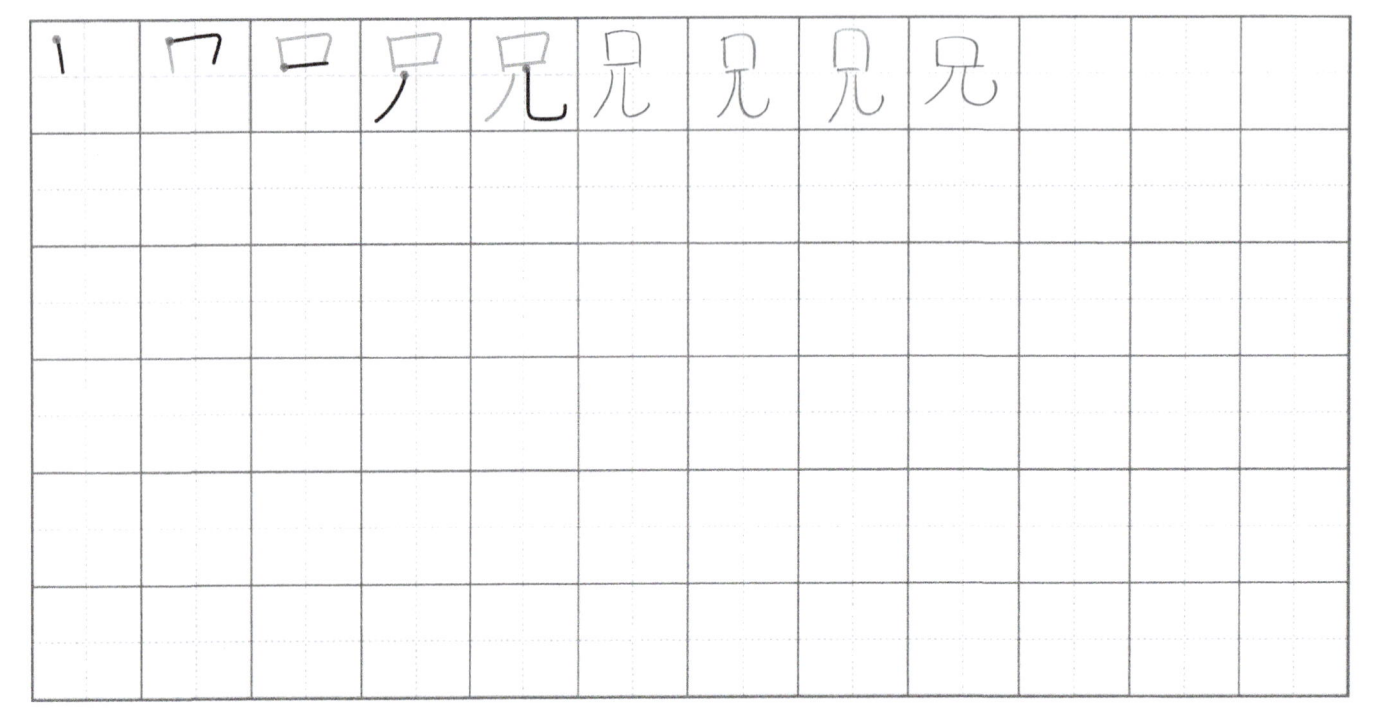

元、兄

光

light; ray

onyomi　コウ
kunyomi　ひか・る
compounds　光 (ひかり) light; illumination
　　　　　　光る (ひかる) to shine; to glitter

公

governmental; public

onyomi　ク、コウ
kunyomi　おおやけ
compounds　公務員 (こうむいん) government worker
　　　　　　公園 (こうえん) park

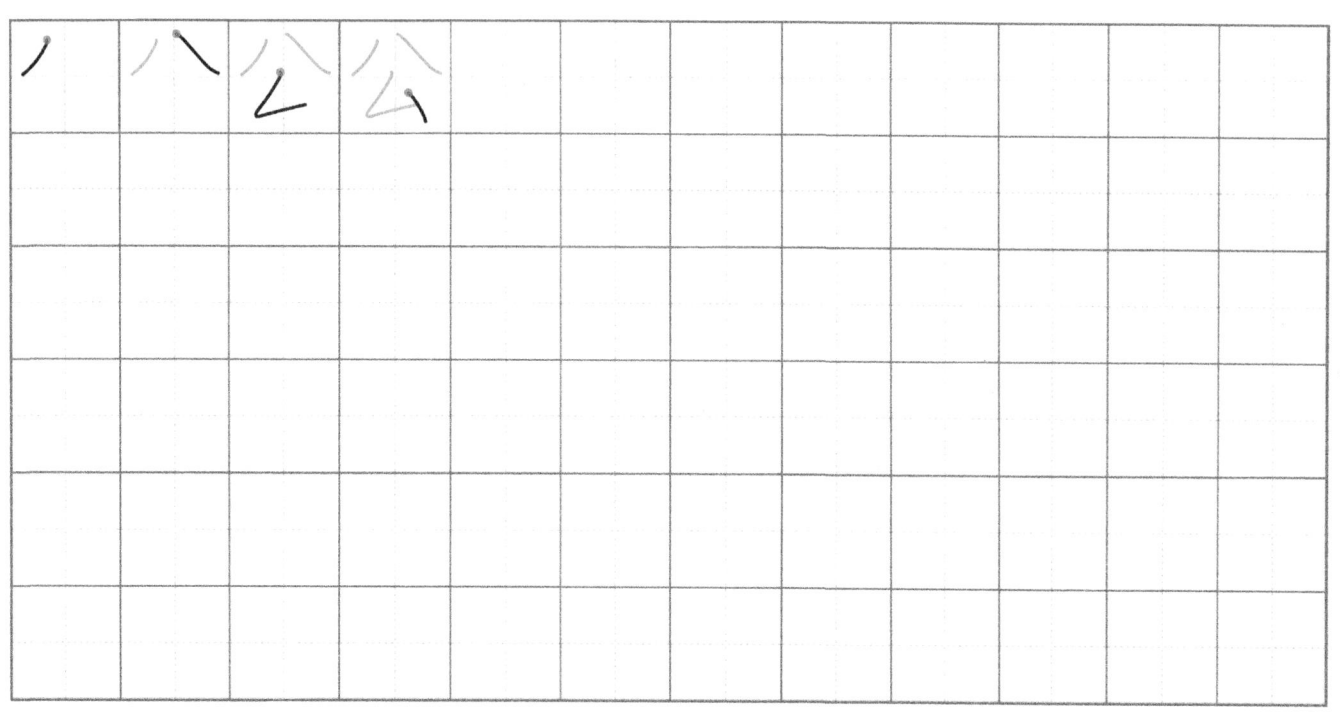

copy

onyomi	シャ、ジャ
kunyomi	うつ・す、うつ・る
compounds	写す（うつす）to copy; to transcribe; to photograph
	写真（しゃしん）photograph; photo; picture

winter

onyomi	トウ
kunyomi	ふゆ
compounds	冬（ふゆ）winter

切

be sharp; cut

onyomi	サイ、セツ
kunyomi	き・る、き・れる
compounds	切る (きる) to cut | to turn off (e.g. the light)
	切符 (きっぷ) ticket
	大切 (たいせつ) important; necessary
	親切 (しんせつ) kindness; gentleness

一　七　切　切

別

branch off; fork; separate

onyomi	ベツ
kunyomi	わか・れる、わ・ける
compounds	別 (べつ) different; another; separate
	別れる (わかれる) to part from; to break up
	特別 (とくべつ) special

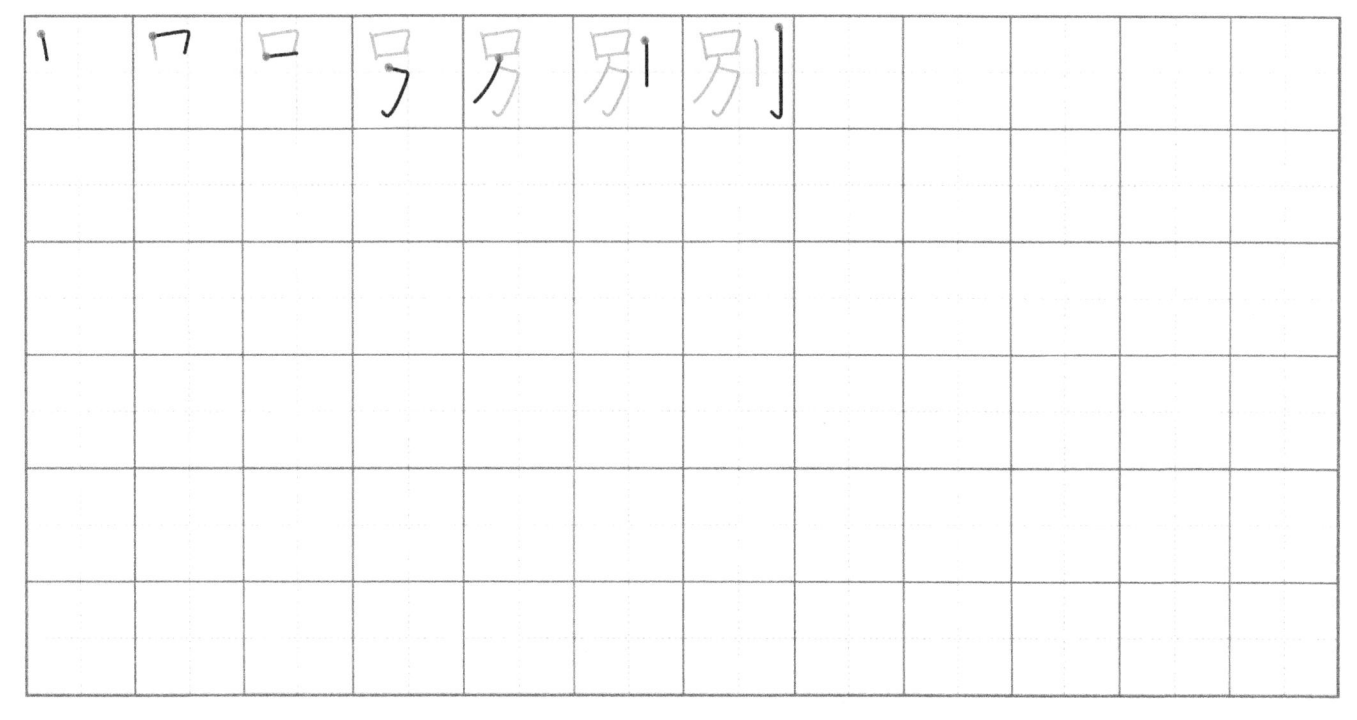

丨　冂　口　号　另　別　別

力

power; strength

onyomi	リイ、リキ、リョク
kunyomi	ちから
compounds	力（ちから）strength; power; skill

勉

diligent; make effort; strive

onyomi	ベン
kunyomi	つと・める
compounds	勉強（べんきょう）study

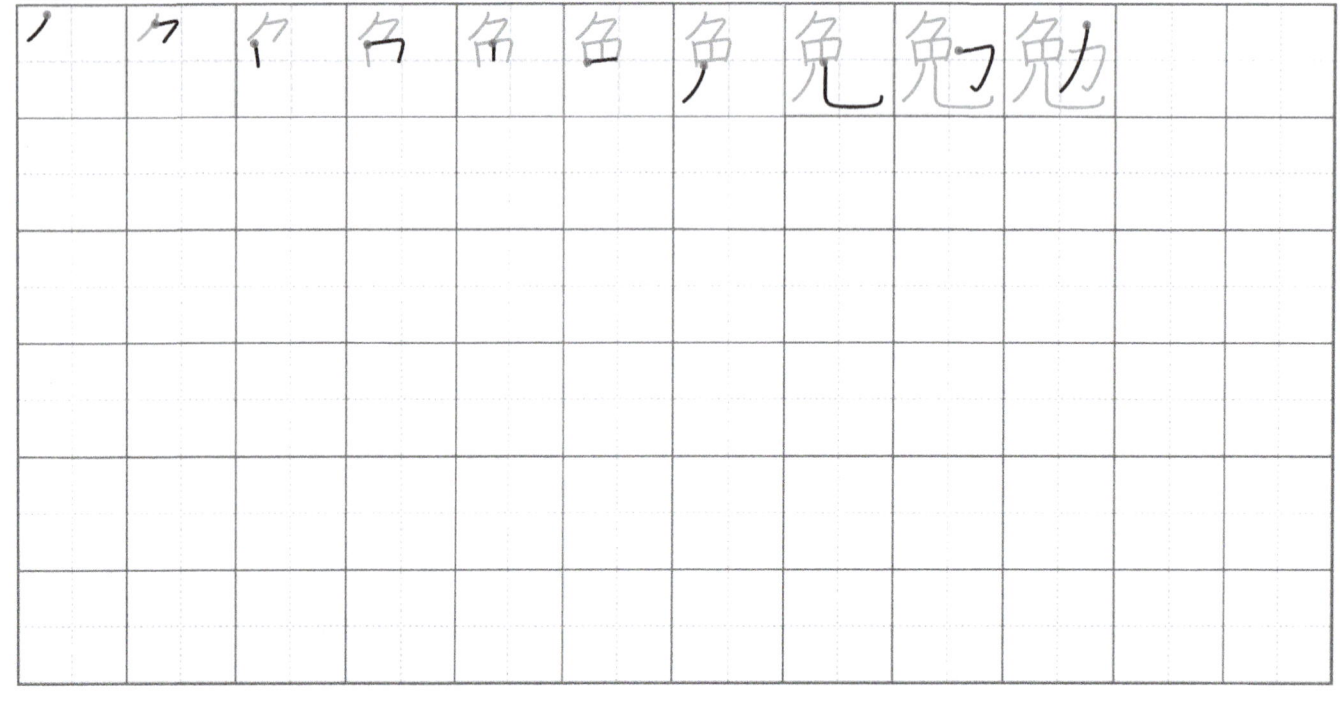

動

change; confusion; motion; move; shake; shift

onyomi ドウ
kunyomi うご・かす、うご・く
compounds 動物（どうぶつ）animal
動物園（どうぶつえん）zoo
自動車（じどうしゃ）automobile
運動（うんどう）exercise; physical training

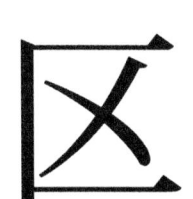

区

district; ward

onyomi ク、コウ
kunyomi
compounds 〜区（〜く）〜 district
渋谷区（しぶやく）(district of) Shibuya

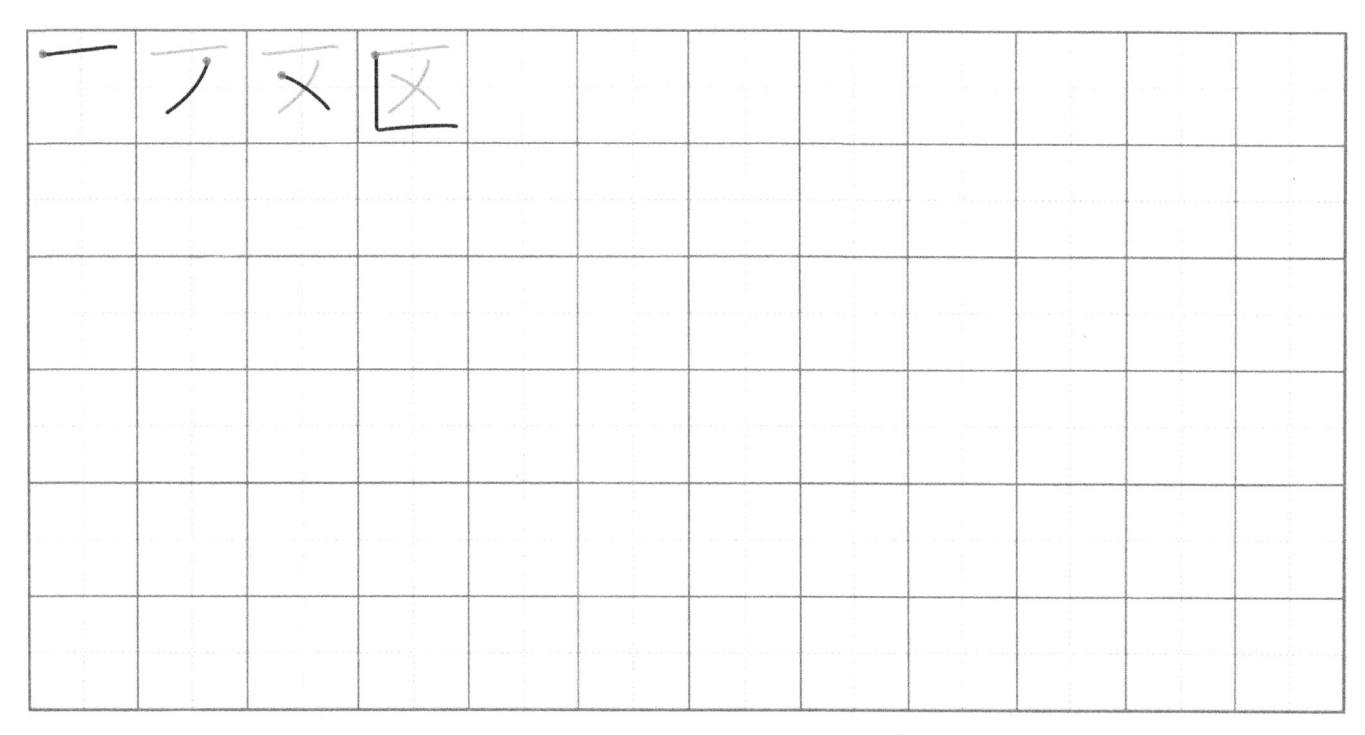

医

doctor; medicine

onyomi　イ
kunyomi　い・する、い・やす
compounds　医学 (いがく) medical science; medicine
　　　　　　医者 (いしゃ) doctor
　　　　　　歯医者 (はいしゃ) dentist

去

eliminate; leave; past; quit

onyomi　キョ、コ
kunyomi　さ・る
compounds　去年 (きょねん) last year

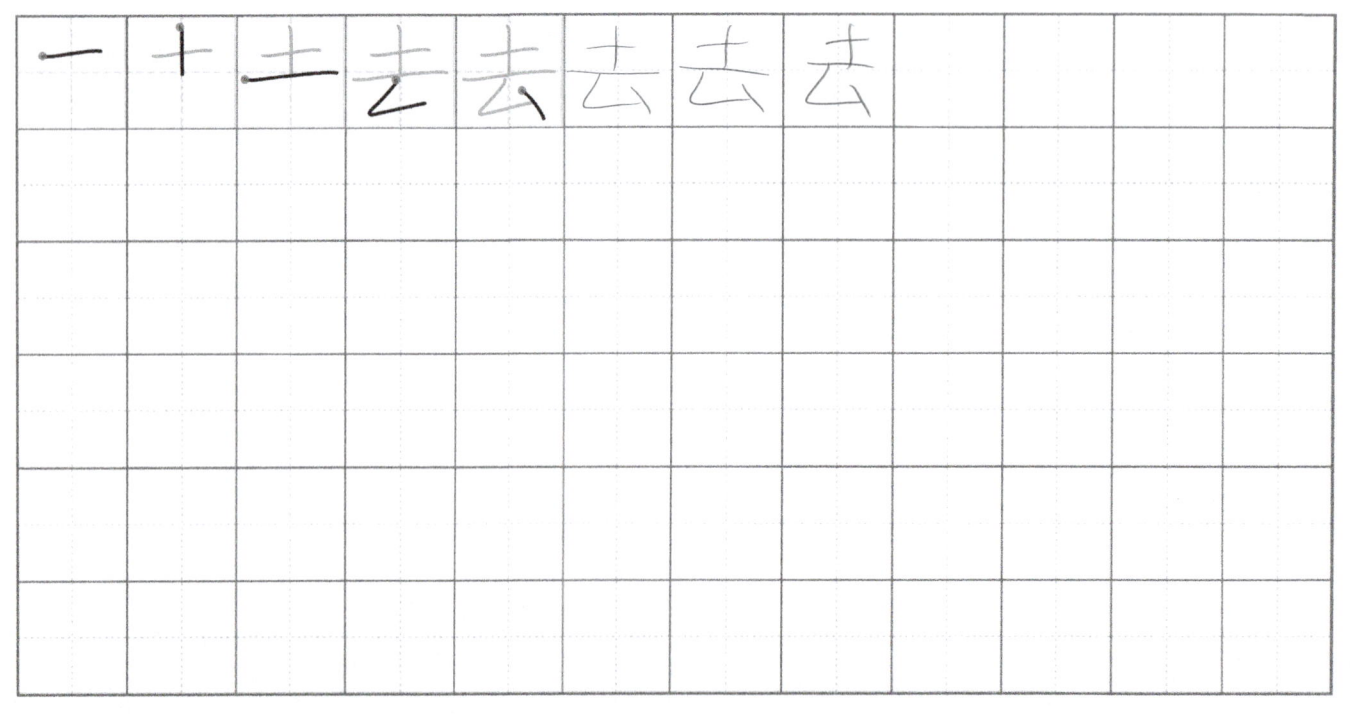

口 mouth

onyomi　ク、コウ
kunyomi　くち
compounds　人口 (じんこう) population
　　　　　　入口 (いりぐち) entrance; entry
　　　　　　出口 (でぐち) exit
　　　　　　口 (くち) mouth | opening; hole

古 old

onyomi　コ
kunyomi　ふる・い
compounds　古い (ふるい) old (not person); aged; stale

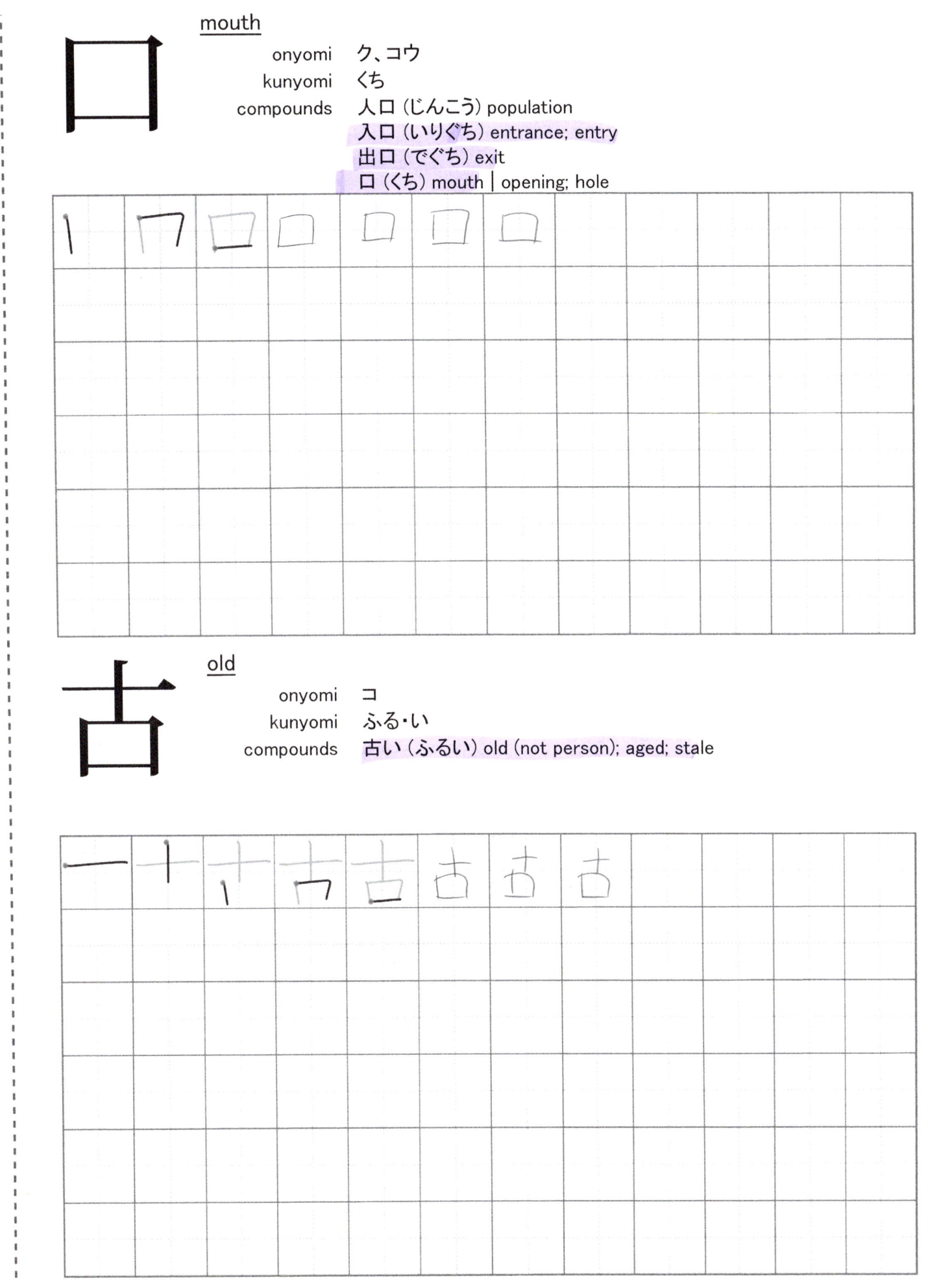

台

onyomi	タイ、ダイ	
kunyomi	つかさ	
compounds	台所 (だいどころ) kitchen	
	台風 (たいふう) typhoon; hurricane	
	〜台 (〜だい) counter for large objects (esp. devices such as refrigerators, cars)	

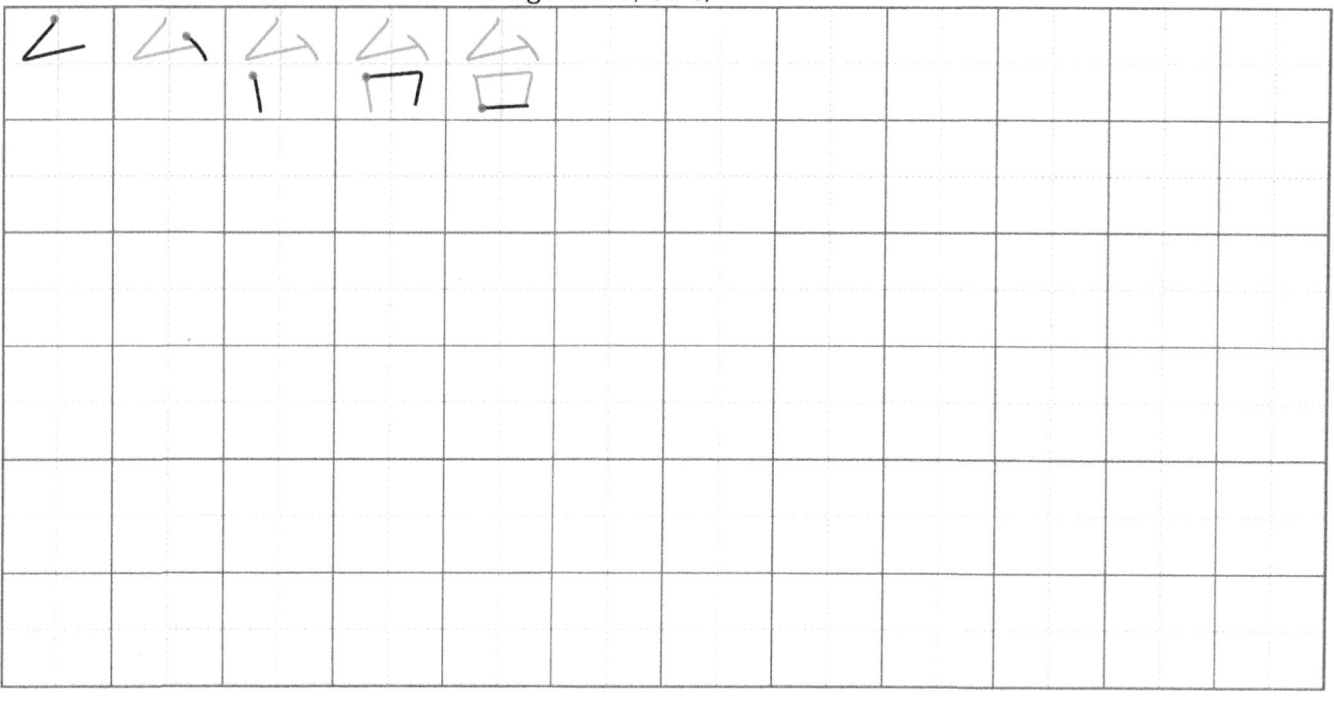

合

fit; join

onyomi	カッ、ガッ、ゴウ	
kunyomi	あ・う、あ・わせる	
compounds	場合 (ばあい) case; situation	
	試合 (しあい) match; game	
	都合 (つごう) circumstances; condition | arrangement	
	間に合う (まにあう) to be in time for	

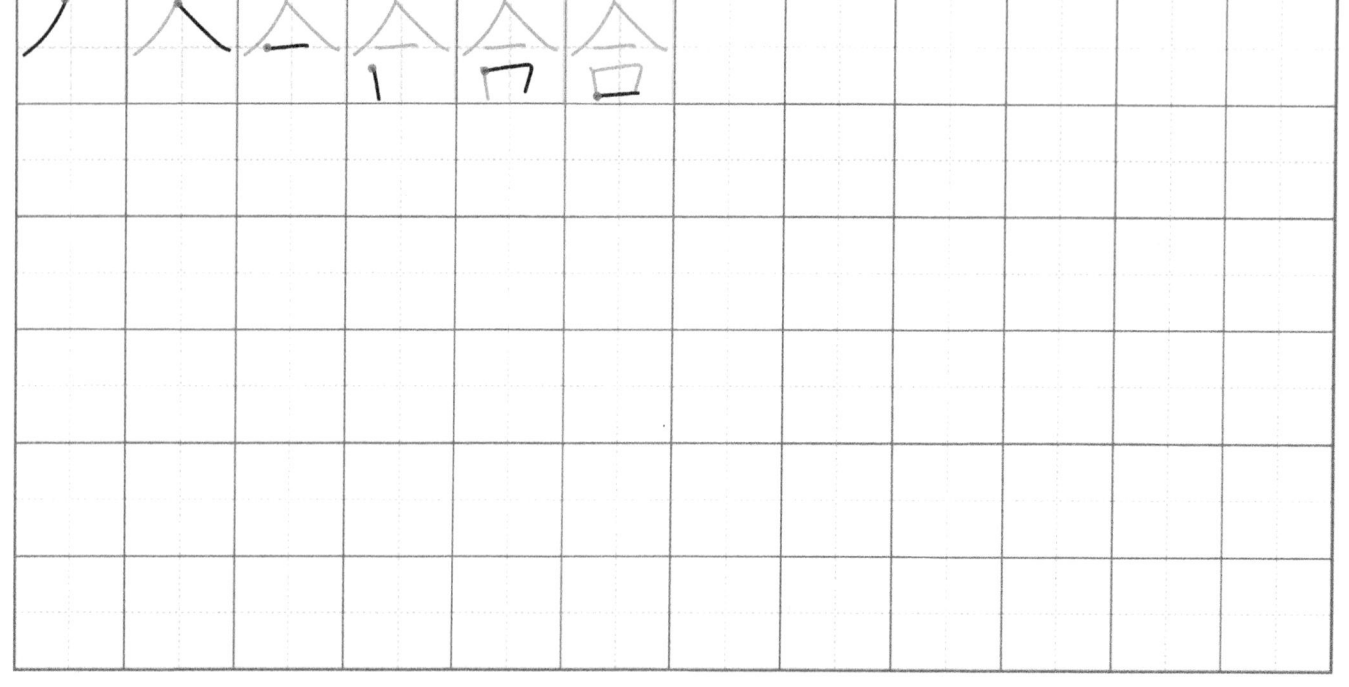

同

agree; equal; same

onyomi	ドウ
kunyomi	おな・じ
compounds	同じ（おなじ）same; identical; equivalent

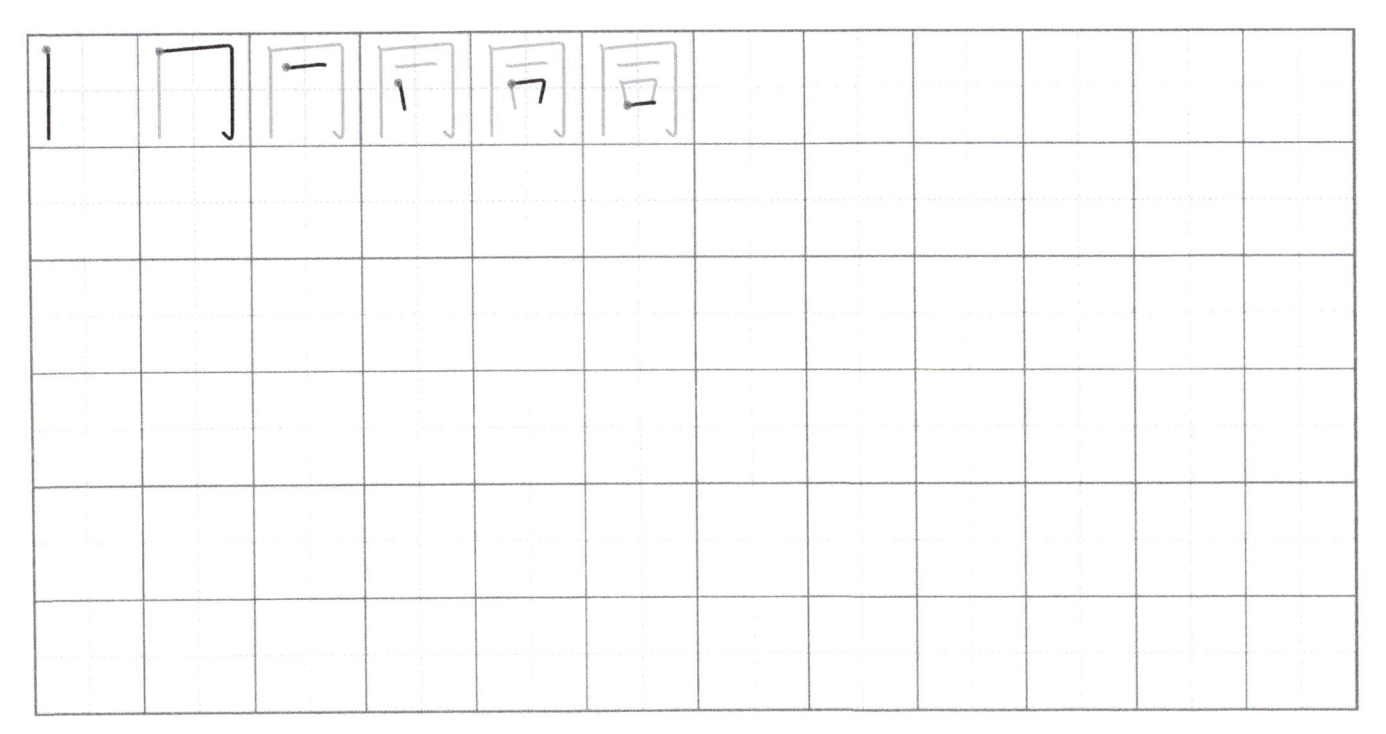

味

flavor; taste

onyomi	ミ
kunyomi	あじ、あじ・わう
compounds	味噌（みそ）(food) miso
	意味（いみ）meaning
	興味（きょうみ）interest (in something); curiosity
	趣味（しゅみ）hobby

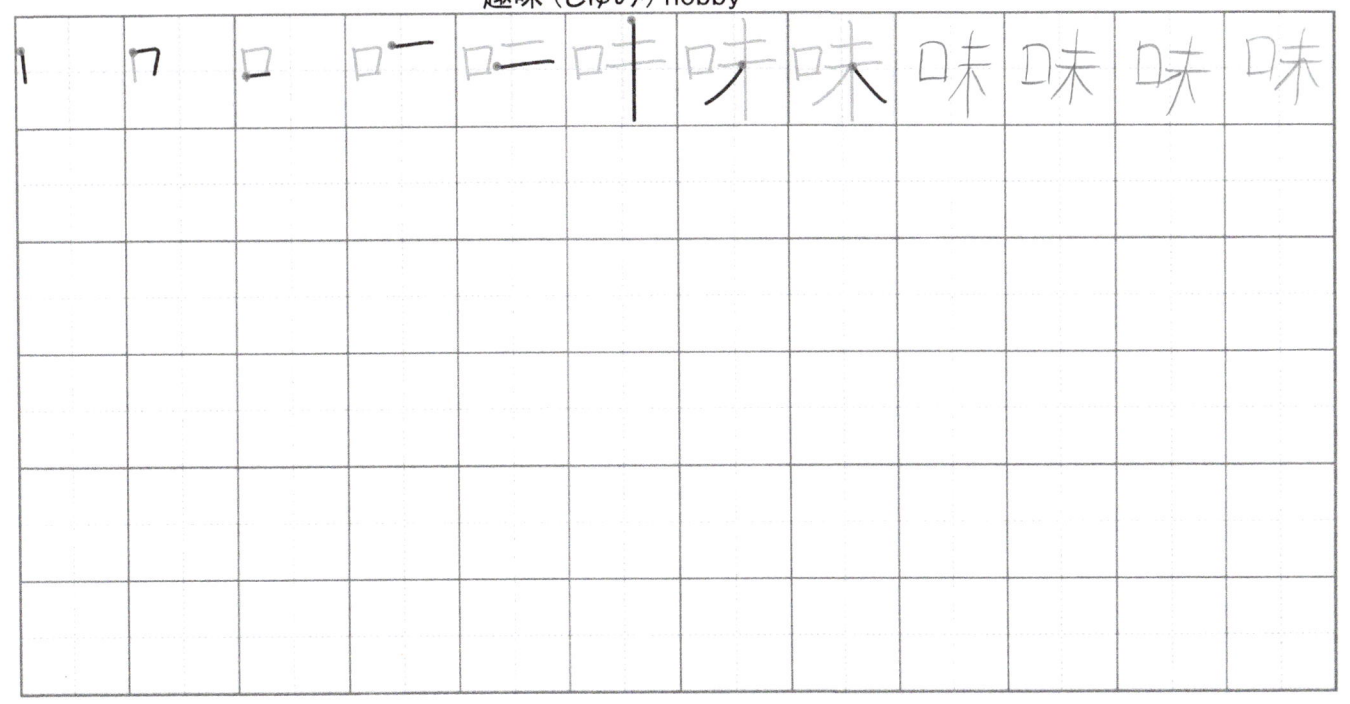

品

goods; refinement

onyomi ヒン
kunyomi しな
compounds 品物 (しなもの) goods; article
食料品 (しょくりょうひん) foodstuff; groceries

員

employee; member

onyomi イン
kunyomi
compounds 会社員 (かいしゃいん) company employee
公務員 (こうむいん) government worker
店員 (てんいん) clerk; salesperson
〜員 (〜いん) member of 〜

問

ask; problem; question

onyomi	モン
kunyomi	と・う
compounds	問題 (もんだい) question (e.g. on a test); problem
	質問 (しつもん) question; inquiry

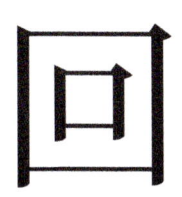

回

~ times; revolve

onyomi	カイ
kunyomi	まわ・す、まわ・る
compounds	回る (まわる) to turn; to revolve; to go around
	～回 (～かい) counter for number of times

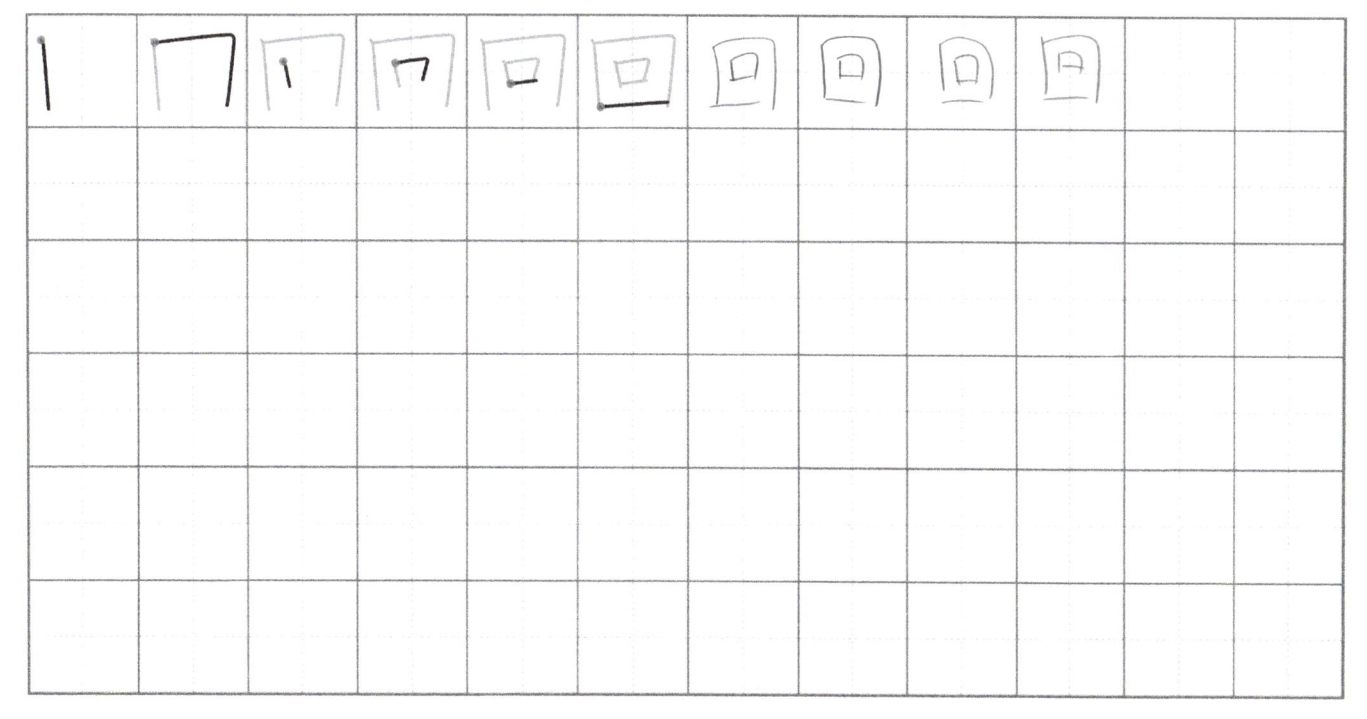

図

onyomi　ズ、ト
kunyomi　はか・る
compounds　図書館 (としょかん) library
　　　　　　地図 (ちず) map

地

earth; ground

onyomi　ジ、チ
kunyomi
compounds　地下鉄 (ちかてつ) subway
　　　　　　地図 (ちず) map
　　　　　　地理 (ちり) geography
　　　　　　地震 (じしん) earthquake

堂

hall

onyomi ドウ

kunyomi

compounds 講堂（こうどう）auditorium; lecture hall
食堂（しょくどう）cafeteria

場

location; place

onyomi ジョウ

kunyomi ば

compounds 会場（かいじょう）assembly hall; venue
場合（ばあい）case; situation
場所（ばしょ）place; location
駐車場（ちゅうしゃじょう）parking lot

声

voice

onyomi	ショウ、セイ
kunyomi	こえ
compounds	声 (こえ) voice

一 十 士 吉 吉 声 声

売

sell

onyomi	バイ
kunyomi	う・る、う・れる
compounds	売り場 (うりば) place where things are sold (sales counter, corner, etc.)
	売る (うる) to sell

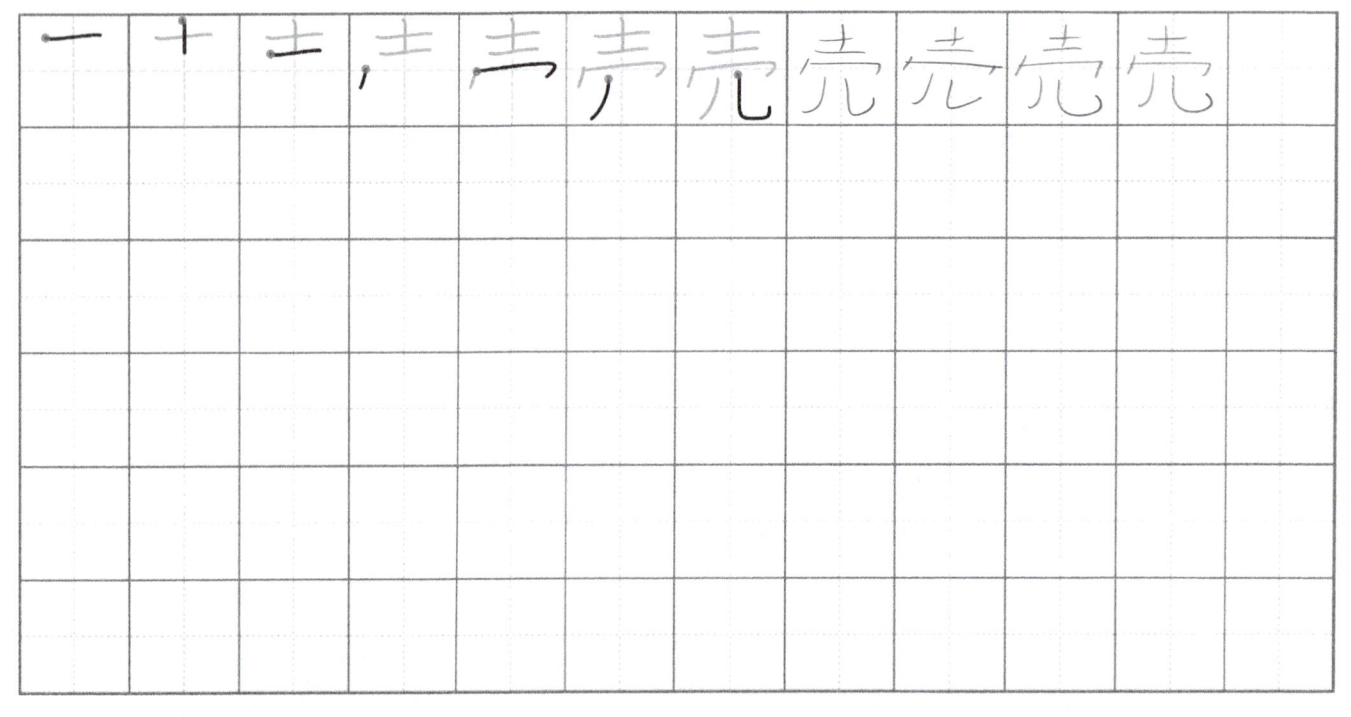

一 十 士 吉 声 声 売 売 売 売 売

声、売   24

夏
summer

onyomi カ、ガ
kunyomi なつ
compounds 夏 (なつ) summer
夏休み (なつやすみ) summer vacation

一	丆	下	百	百	百	百	夏	夏	夏	夏	夏
夏											

夕
evening

onyomi
kunyomi ゆう
compounds 夕方 (ゆうがた) evening; dusk
夕飯 (ゆうめし、ゆうはん) evening meal

ノ	ク	夕	夕	夕	夕	夕	夕	夕	夕	夕	夕

多

onyomi タ
kunyomi おお・い
compounds 多い（おおい）many; a lot | large quantity
多分（たぶん）perhaps; probably

夜

evening

onyomi ヤ
kunyomi よ、よる
compounds 今夜（こんや）this evening; tonight
夜（よる）evening; night
昨夜（ゆうべ）last night

多、夜

太

plump; thick

onyomi	タ、タイ
kunyomi	ふと・い、ふと・る
compounds	太い（ふとい）fat; thick | deep (of a voice)
	太る（ふとる）to become fat

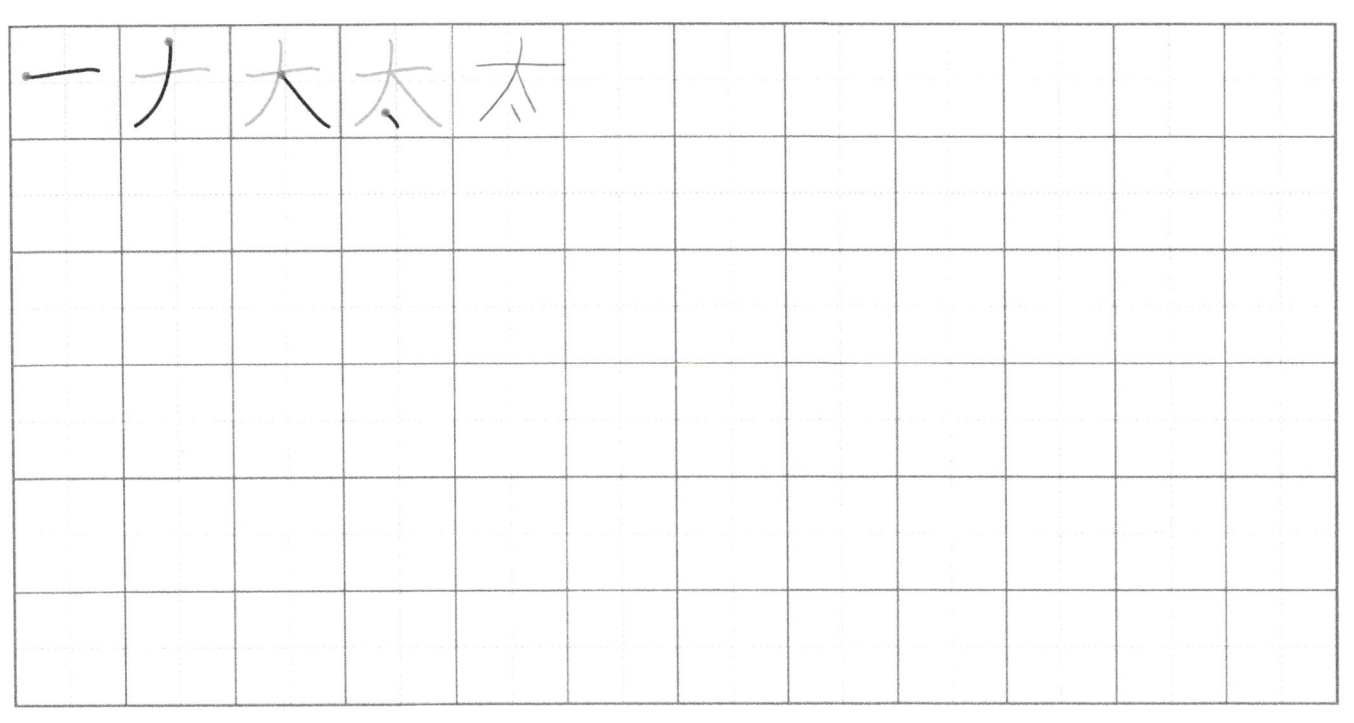

好

fond; pleasing

onyomi	コウ
kunyomi	この・む、す・く
compounds	大好き（だいすき）loveable; like very much
	好き（すき）like; likable

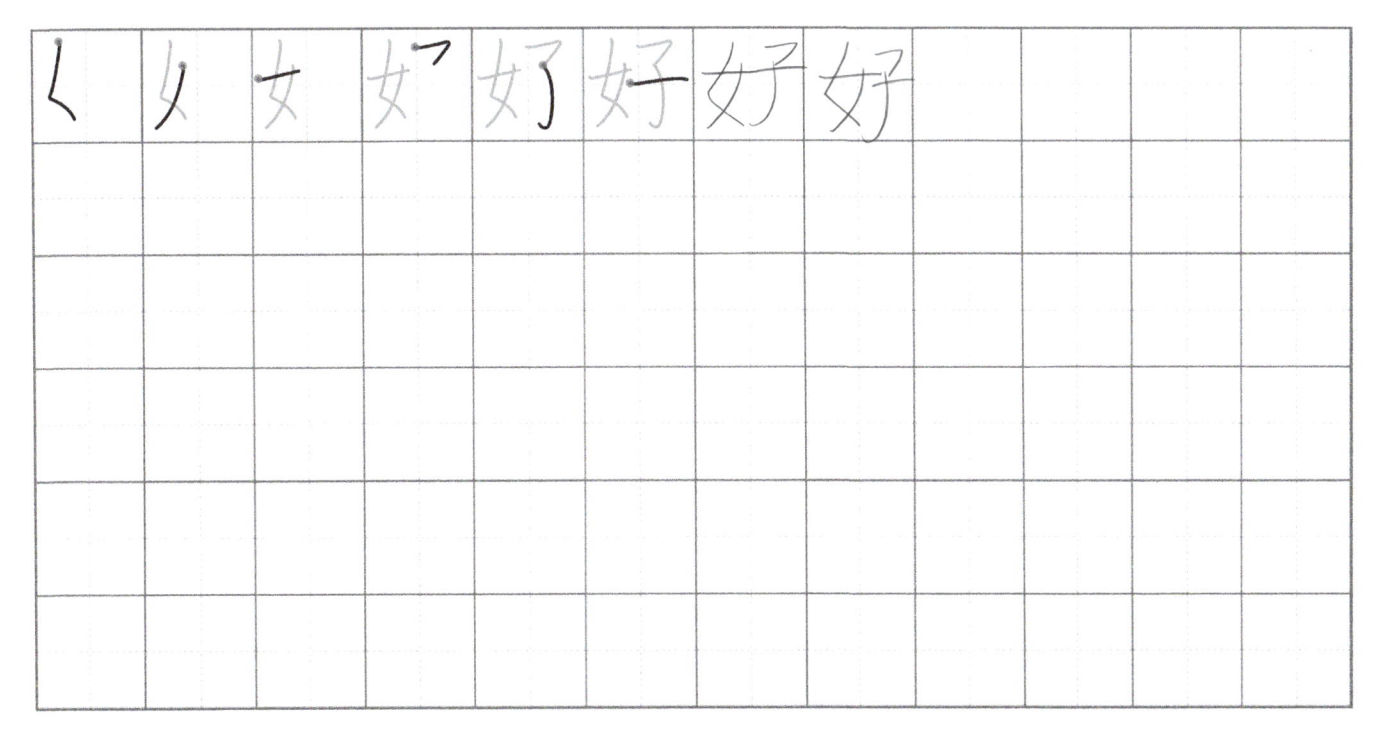

妹

onyomi　マイ
kunyomi　いもうと
compounds　妹 (いもうと) (hum) younger sister

姉

elder sister

onyomi　シ
kunyomi　あね
compounds　お姉さん (おねえさん) elder sister
　　　　　　姉 (あね) (hum) older sister

妹、姉

begin

onyomi	シ
kunyomi	はじ・まる、はじ・める
compounds	始まる (はじまる) to begin; to start
	始める (はじめる) to start; to begin

character; letter

onyomi	ジ
kunyomi	あざ
compounds	字 (じ) character; letter | hand-writing
	字引き (じびき) dictionary
	漢字 (かんじ) Chinese characters; kanji

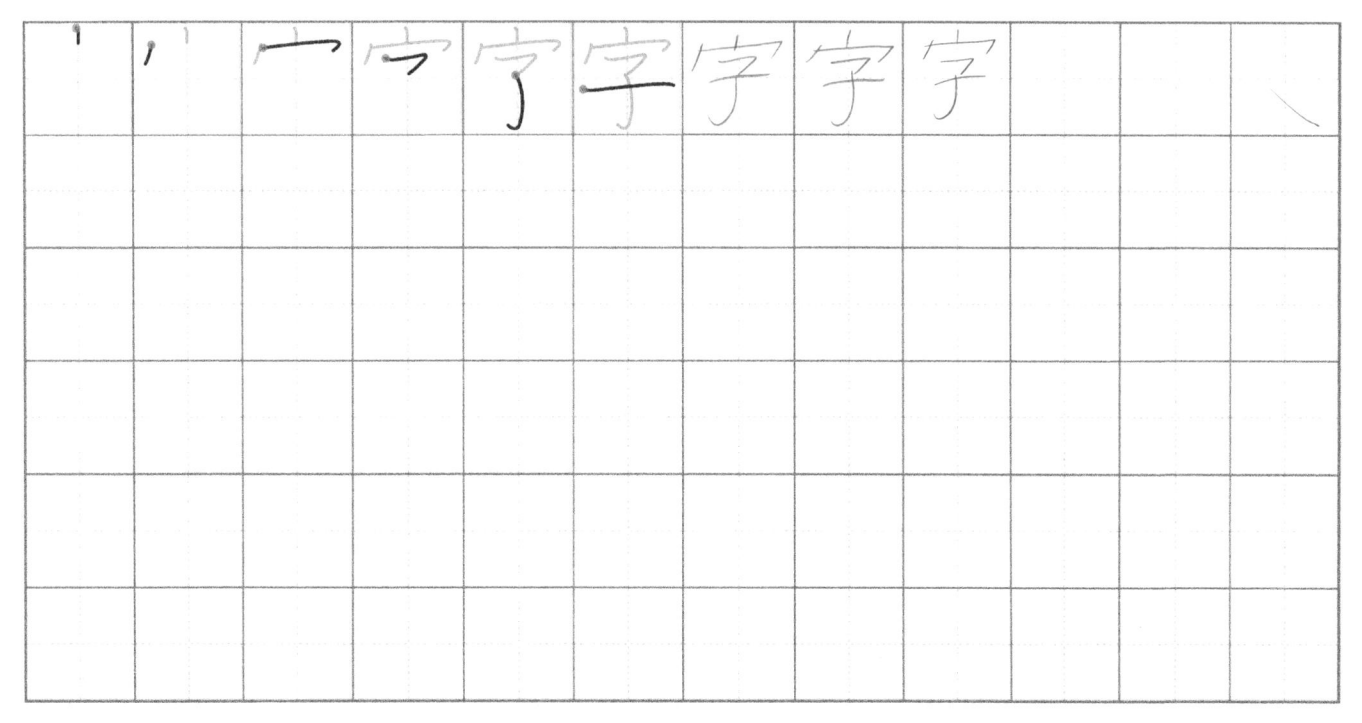

cheap; peaceful; relaxed

onyomi	アン
kunyomi	やす・い、やす・まる
compounds	安い (やすい) cheap; inexpensive
	安全 (あんぜん) safety; security
	安心 (あんしん) relief; peace of mind

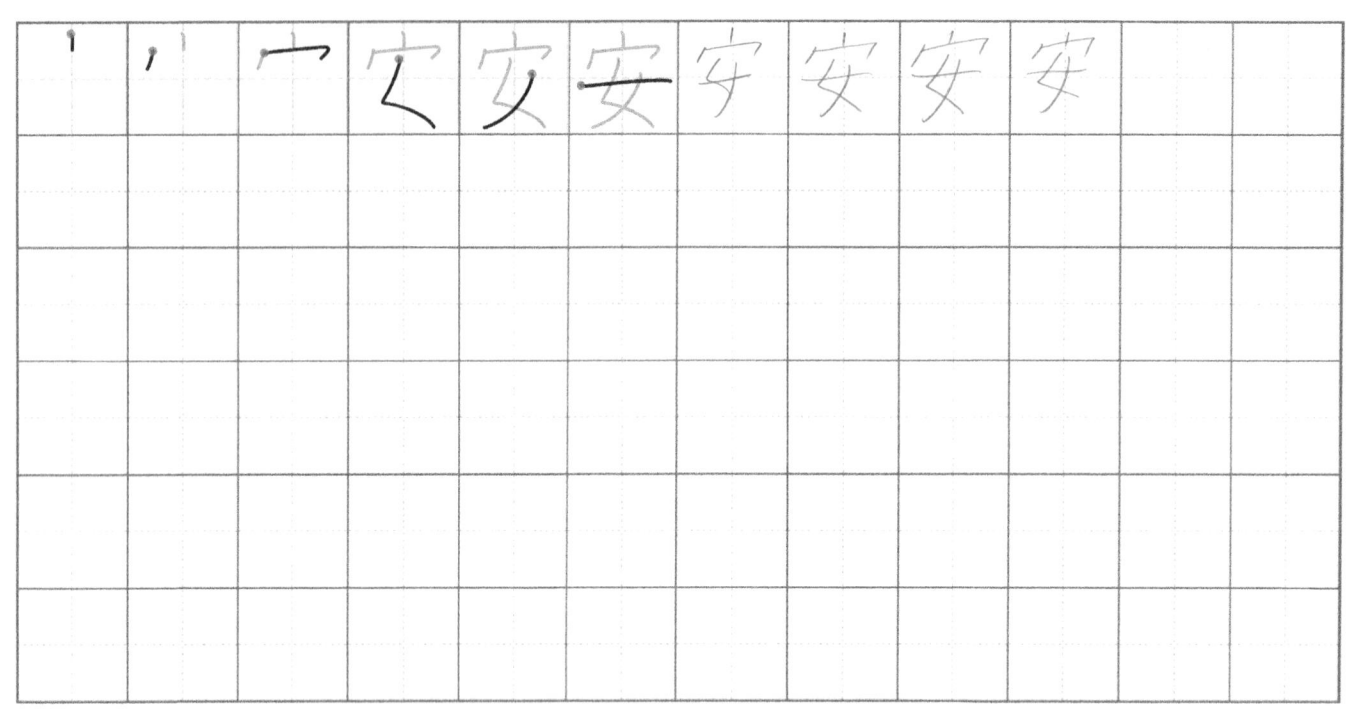

chamber; room

onyomi	シツ
kunyomi	
compounds	会議室 (かいぎしつ) conference room
	教室 (きょうしつ) classroom
	研究室 (けんきゅうしつ) laboratory

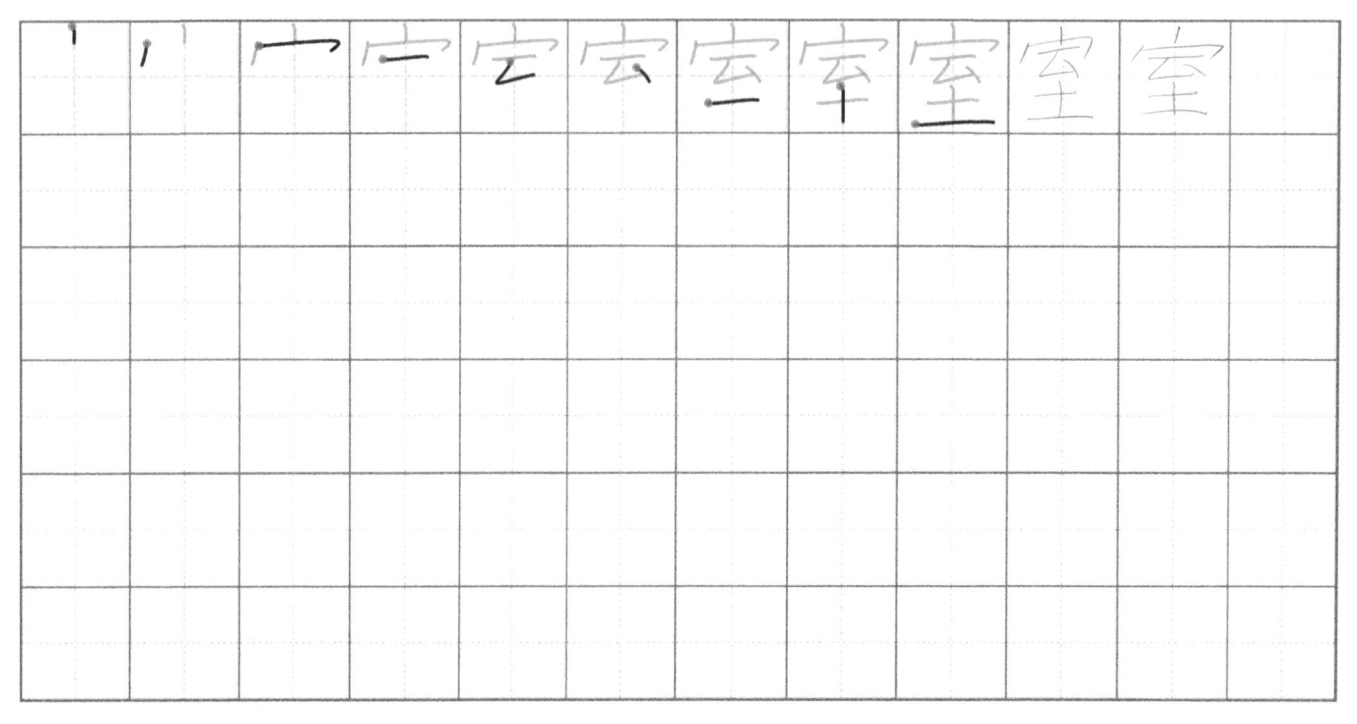

安、室

家

family; home; expert; professional

onyomi カ、ケ
kunyomi いえ、うち、や
compounds 家（いえ、うち）house; residence; dwelling
家内（かない）(hum) wife | one's family
家庭（かてい）household; family
家族（かぞく）family; members of a family

寒

cold

onyomi カン
kunyomi さむ・い
compounds 寒い（さむい）cold (e.g. weather)

少

few

onyomi	ショウ
kunyomi	すく・ない、すこ・し
compounds	少し（すこし）small quantity; little; few
	少ない（すくない）few; a little

屋

house; roof; shop

onyomi	オク
kunyomi	や
compounds	八百屋（やおや）greengrocer
	屋上（おくじょう）rooftop
	部屋（へや）room

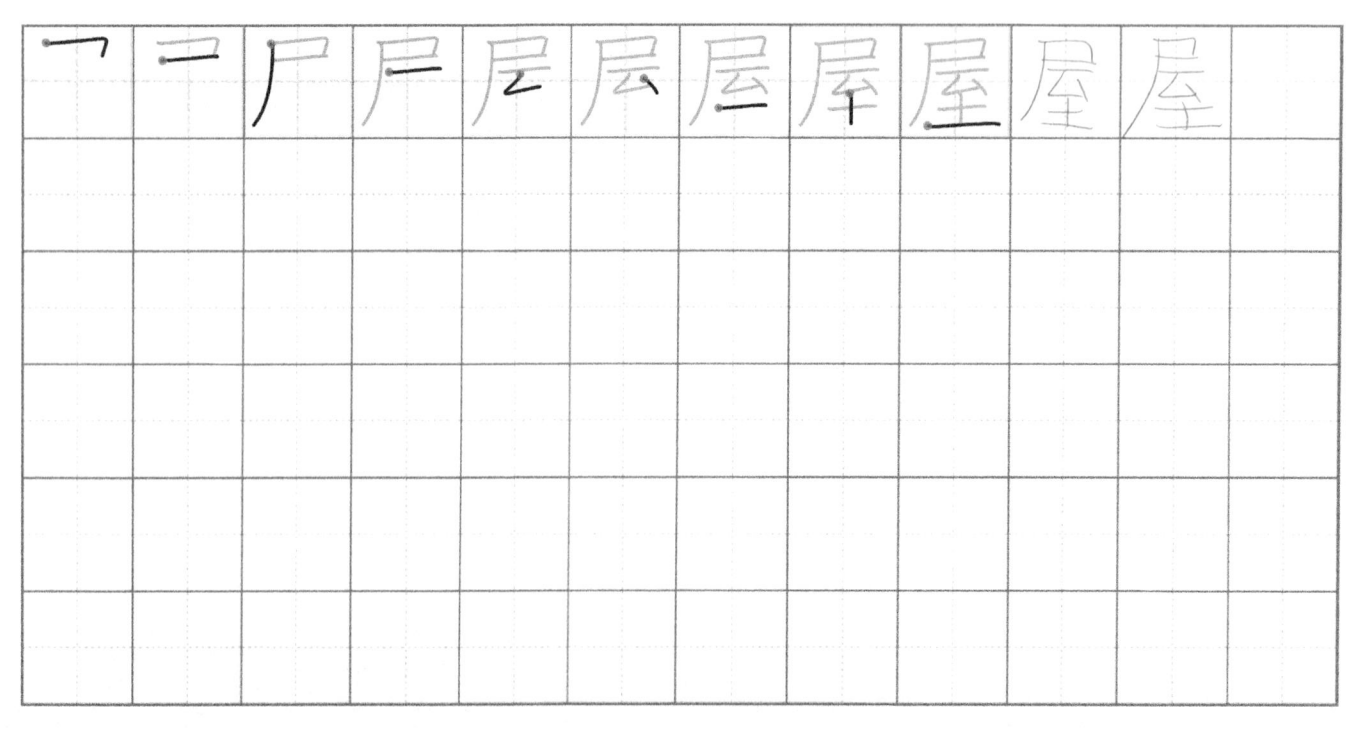

少、屋

工

construction; craft; katakana e radical (no. 48)

onyomi　ク、コウ

kunyomi

compounds　工場 (こうじょう、こうば) factory; plant; mill; workshop
工業 (こうぎょう) industry; industrial

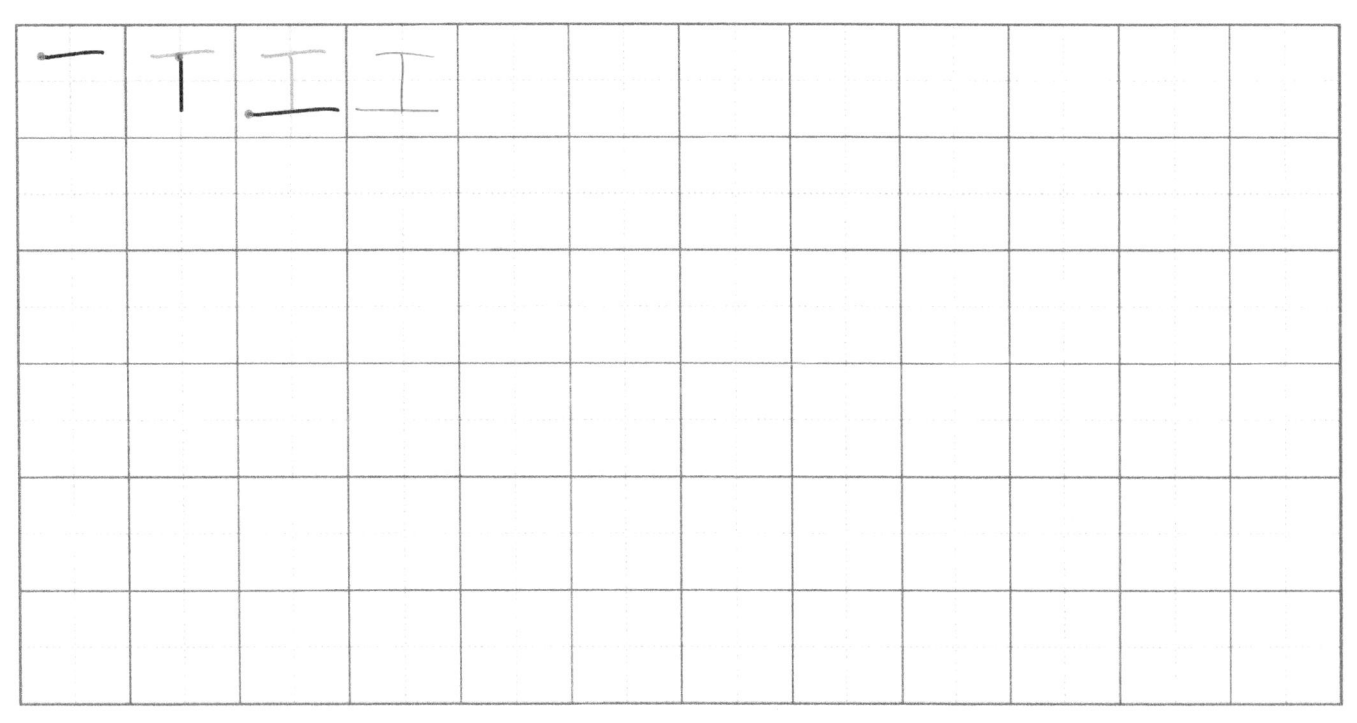

市

city; market

onyomi　シ

kunyomi　いち

compounds　市 (し) city
市民 (しみん) city resident; townspeople

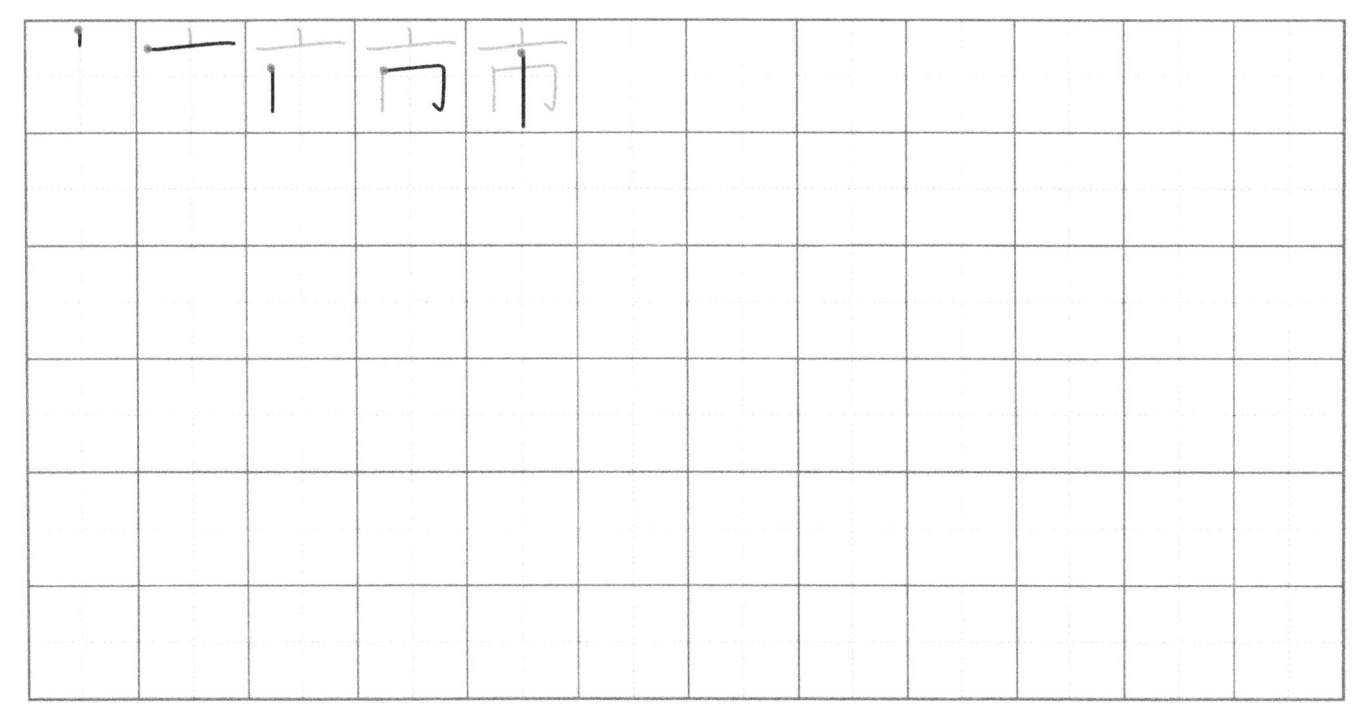

帰

onyomi　キ
kunyomi　かえ・る
compounds　帰り（かえり）return; coming back
　　　　　　帰る（かえる）to return; to come home

広

wide

onyomi　コウ
kunyomi　ひろ・い、ひろ・がる、ひろ・げる、ひろ・まる、ひろ・める
compounds　広い（ひろい）spacious; wide

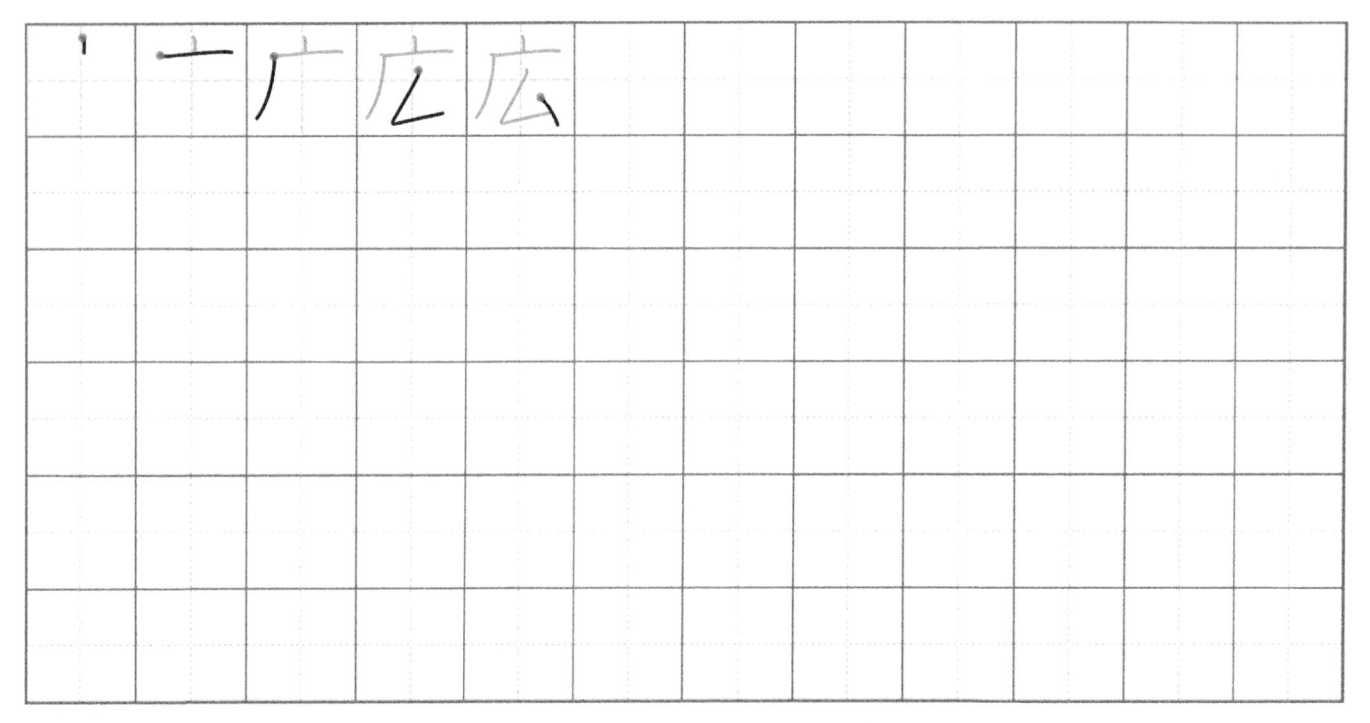

帰、広

34

店

shop; store

onyomi	テン
kunyomi	みせ
compounds	喫茶店 (きっさてん) coffee shop; cafe
	店 (みせ) store; shop
	店員 (てんいん) clerk; salesperson

度

degrees; occurrence; time

onyomi	タク、ド
kunyomi	たび
compounds	もう一度 (もういちど) once more; again
	今度 (こんど) next time; another time
	支度 (したく) preparation; arrangements
	〜度 (〜ど) counter for number of times

建 build

onyomi　ケン
kunyomi　た・つ、た・てる
compounds　建てる (たてる) to build; to construct
　　　　　　建物 (たてもの) building
　　　　　　〜階建て (〜かいだて) 〜-storied building

引 pull

onyomi　イン
kunyomi　ひ・く、ひ・ける
compounds　字引き (じびき) dictionary
　　　　　　引き出し (ひきだし) drawer
　　　　　　引き出す (ひきだす) to pull out; to bring out; to withdraw
　　　　　　引っ越す (ひっこす) to move; to change residence

弟

younger brother

onyomi　ダイ
kunyomi　おとうと
compounds　兄弟 (きょうだい) siblings; brothers and sisters
　　　　　弟 (おとうと) (hum) younger brother

弱

frail; weak

onyomi　ジャク
kunyomi　よわ・い、よわ・まる、よわ・める
compounds　弱い (よわい) weak; frail

強

onyomi キョウ、ゴウ

kunyomi つよ・い、つよ・まる、つよ・める

compounds 勉強 (べんきょう) study

強い (つよい) strong; powerful

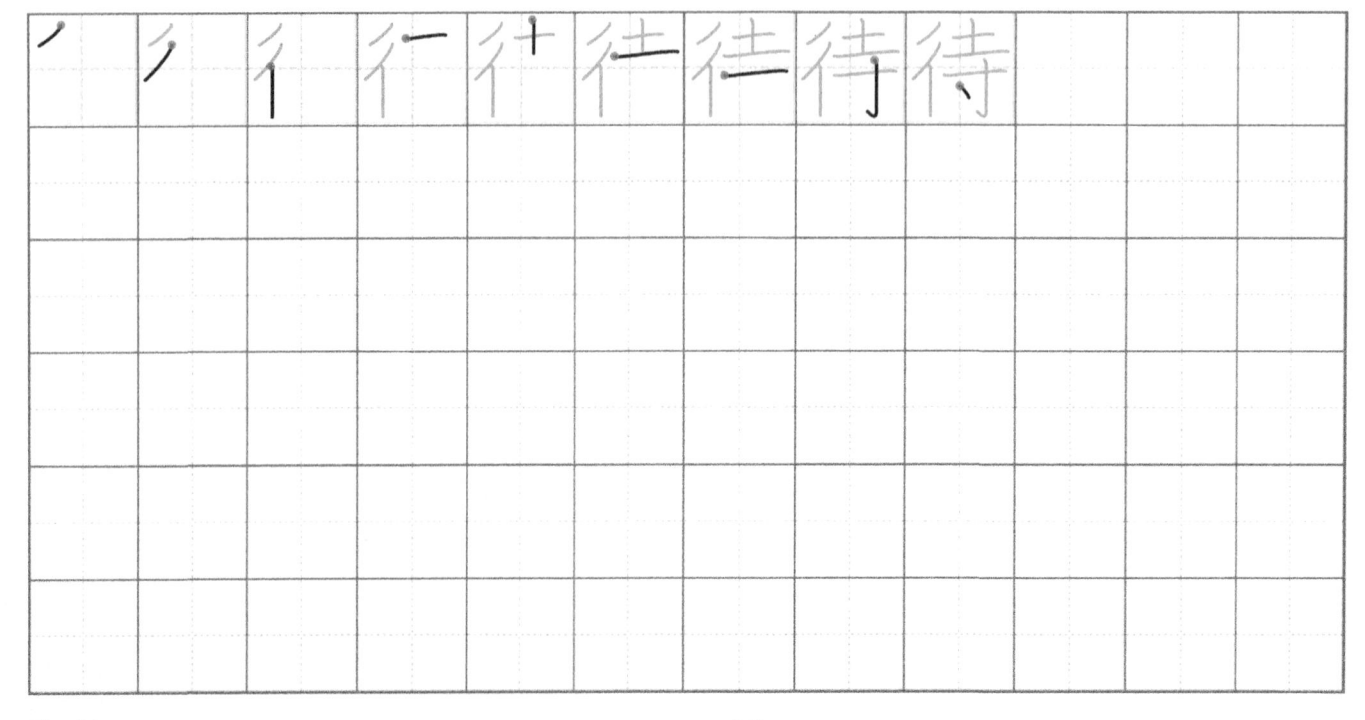

待

depend on; wait

onyomi タイ

kunyomi ま・つ

compounds 待つ (まつ) to wait

招待 (しょうたい) invitation

心

heart; mind; spirit

onyomi	シン
kunyomi	こころ
compounds	心 (こころ) mind; heart; spirit
	安心 (あんしん) relief; peace of mind
	心配 (しんぱい) worry; concern
	熱心 (ねっしん) zeal; enthusiasm

思

think

onyomi	シ
kunyomi	おも・う
compounds	思い出す (おもいだす) to recall; to remember
	思う (おもう) to think

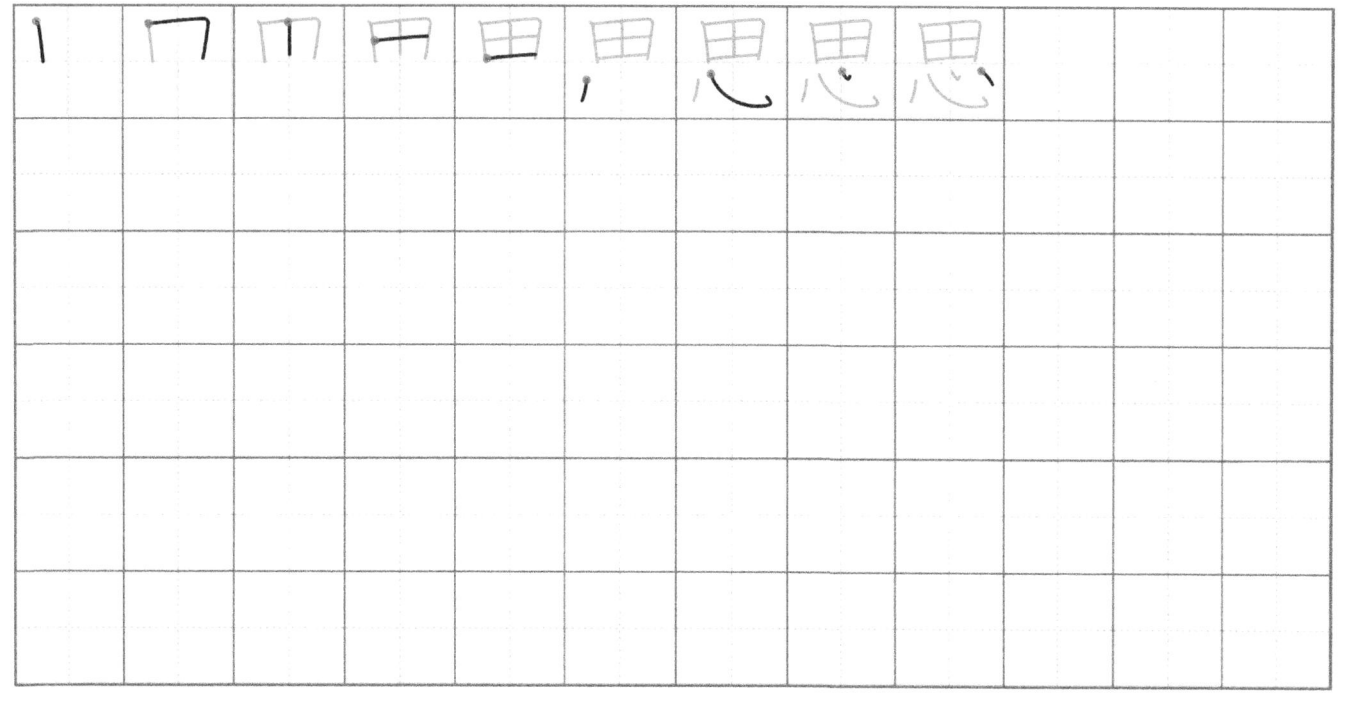

急

emergency; hurry

onyomi　キュウ

kunyomi　いそ・ぎ、いそ・ぐ

compounds　急ぐ (いそぐ) to hurry; to rush

急行 (きゅうこう) express (train)

特急 (とっきゅう) limited express (train, faster than an express)

悪

bad; evil

onyomi　アク

kunyomi　わる・い

compounds　悪い (わるい) bad; poor; inferior | evil; sinful

意

care; desire; thought

onyomi	イ
kunyomi	
compounds	意味 (いみ) meaning
	意見 (いけん) opinion
	注意 (ちゅうい) caution; attention; warning
	用意 (ようい) preparation; arrangements

所

extent; place

onyomi	ショ
kunyomi	ところ、どころ
compounds	事務所 (じむしょ) office
	住所 (じゅうしょ) address (e.g. of house)
	台所 (だいどころ) kitchen
	場所 (ばしょ) place; location

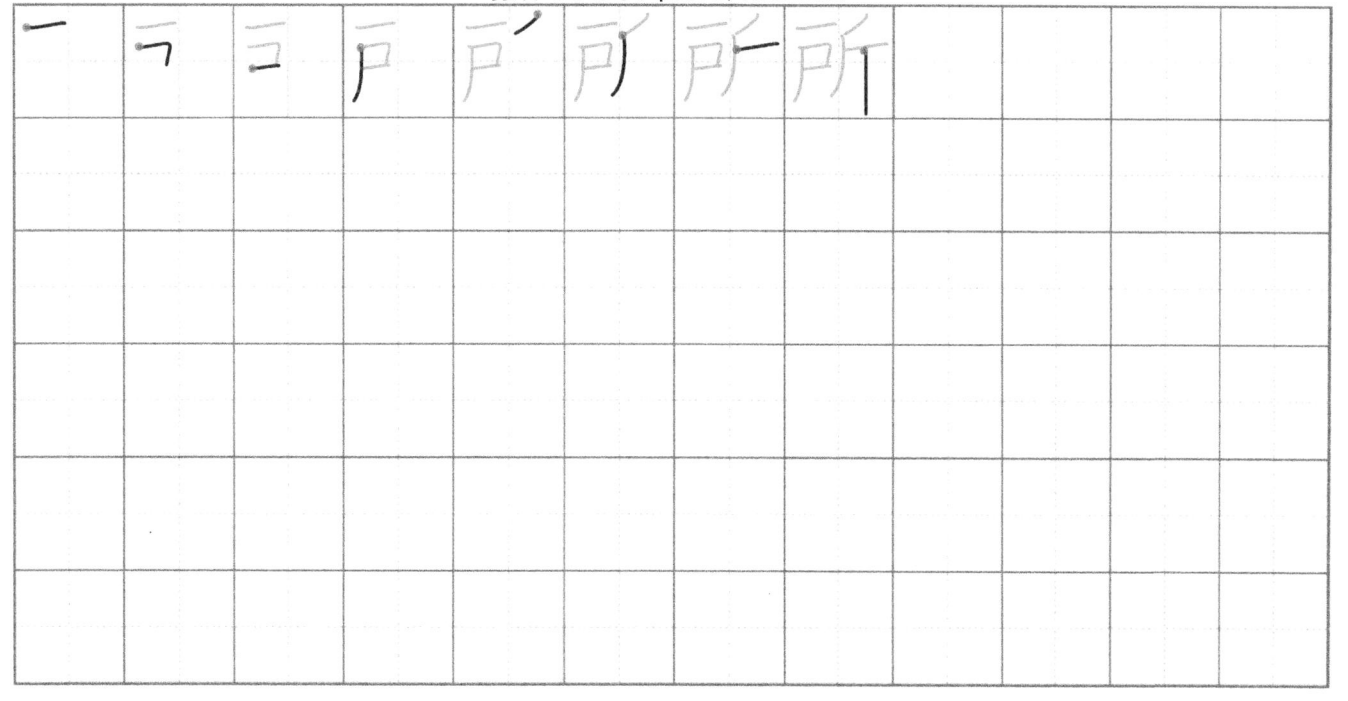

hand

onyomi シュ、ズ

kunyomi て

compounds お手洗い（おてあらい）toilet; restroom
上手（じょうず）skillful; proficient; good (at)
手伝う（てつだう）to help; to assist
手紙（てがみ）letter

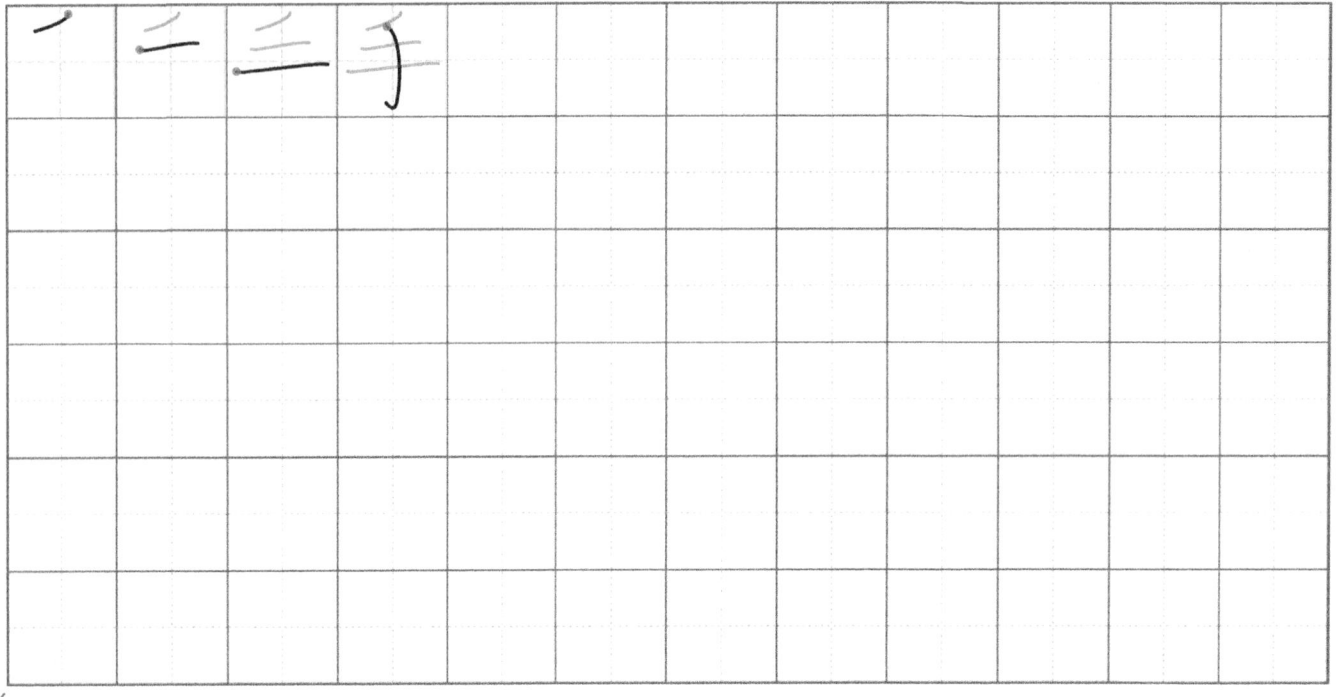

have; hold

onyomi ジ

kunyomi も・つ、も・てる

compounds 持つ（もつ）to hold | to possess; to have
気持ち（きもち）feeling; sensation; mood
金持ち（かねもち）rich person

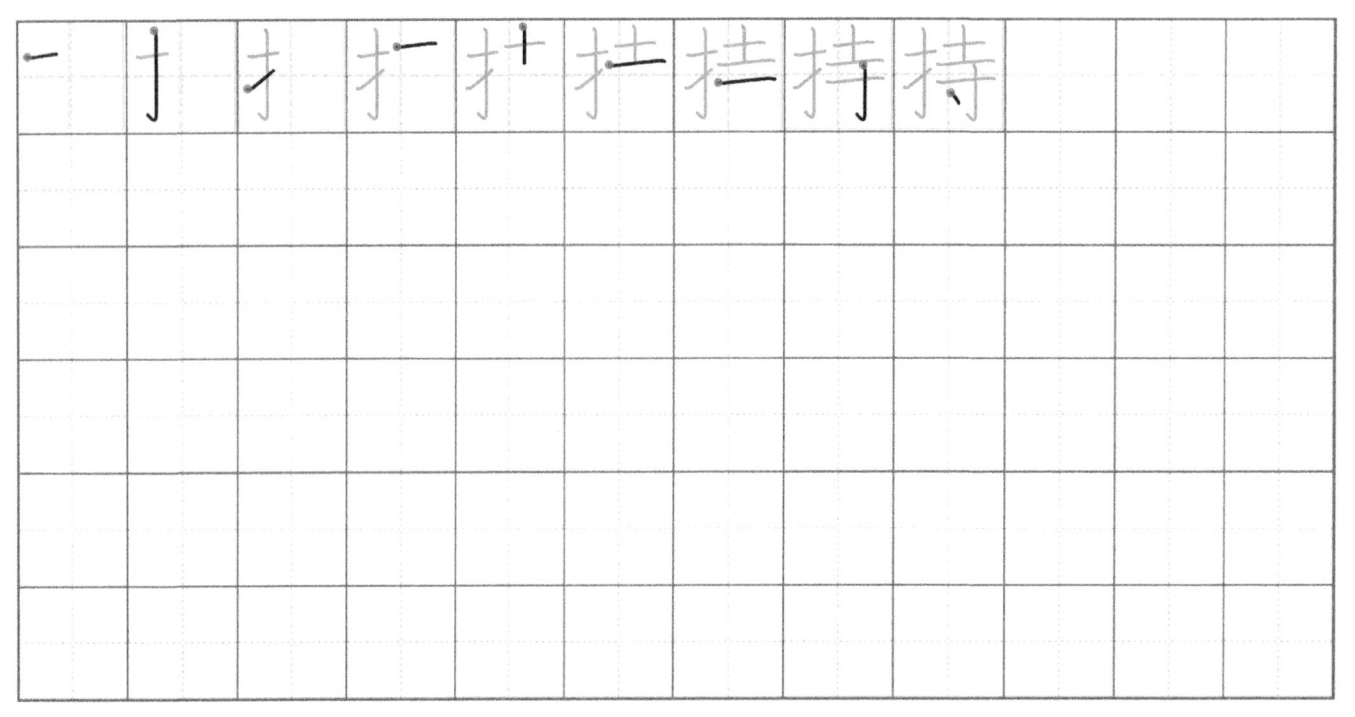

手、持

doctrine; faith; teach

onyomi	キョウ
kunyomi	おし・える、おそ・わる
compounds	教える (おしえる) to teach; to instruct
	教会 (きょうかい) church
	教室 (きょうしつ) classroom
	教育 (きょういく) education; schooling; training

一 十 土 耂 耂 考 孝 孝 教 教 教

art; decoration; literature

onyomi	ブン、モン
kunyomi	あや、ふみ
compounds	作文 (さくぶん) writing; composition
	文化 (ぶんか) culture
	文学 (ぶんがく) literature
	文法 (ぶんぽう) grammar

丶 一 ナ 文

fee; materials

onyomi リョウ

kunyomi

compounds 料理 (りょうり) cooking; cuisine
食料品 (しょくりょうひん) foodstuff; groceries

new

onyomi シン

kunyomi あたら・しい、あら・た

compounds 新しい (あたらしい) new
新聞 (しんぶん) newspaper
新聞社 (しんぶんしゃ) newspaper company

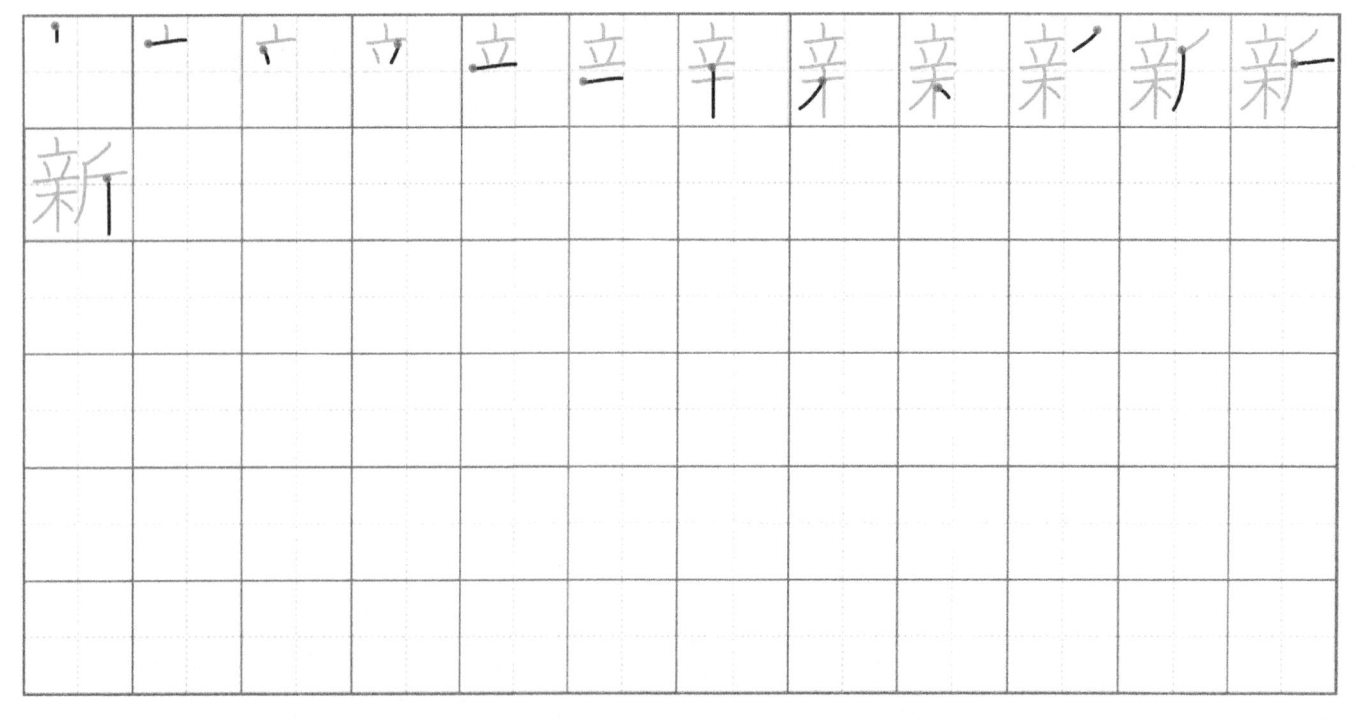

方

onyomi	ホウ
kunyomi	かた
compounds	両方（りょうほう）both; both sides
	仕方（しかた）way; method; means
	夕方（ゆうがた）evening; dusk
	方（かた）(hon) person

旅

travel; trip

onyomi	リョ
kunyomi	たび
compounds	旅行（りょこう）trip
	旅館（りょかん）Japanese-style lodging

族

family; tribe

onyomi　ゾク

kunyomi

compounds　家族（かぞく）family; members of a family

早

early; fast

onyomi　サッ、ソウ

kunyomi　はや・い、はや・まる、はや・める

compounds　早い（はやい）early; fast; quick

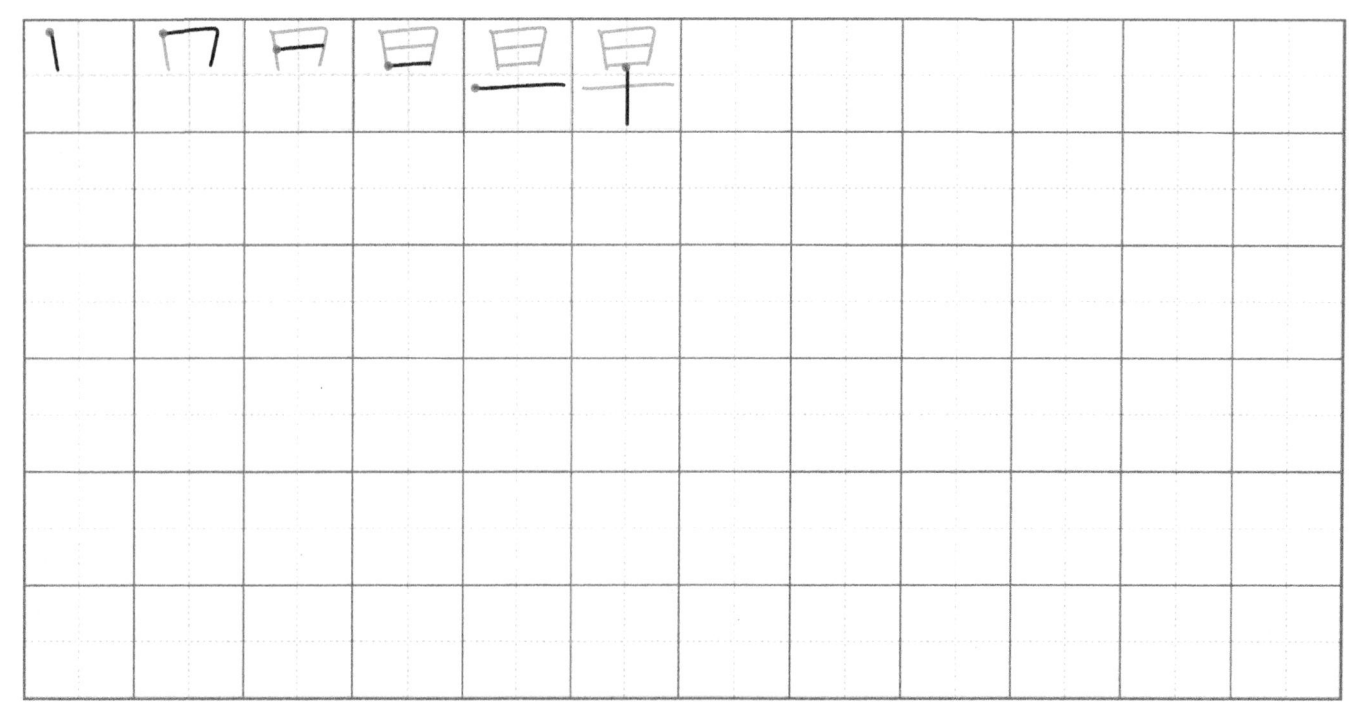

明

bright; light

onyomi	ミョウ、メイ
kunyomi	あか・るい、あき・らか、あ・かり
compounds	明るい（あかるい）bright; colourful
	明日（あした）tomorrow
	明日（あした、あす）tomorrow
	説明（せつめい）explanation; exposition

映

projection; reflection

onyomi	エイ
kunyomi	うつ・す、うつ・る、は・える
compounds	映画（えいが）movie; film
	映画館（えいがかん）movie theatre

春

springtime

onyomi シュン
kunyomi はる
compounds 春 (はる) spring

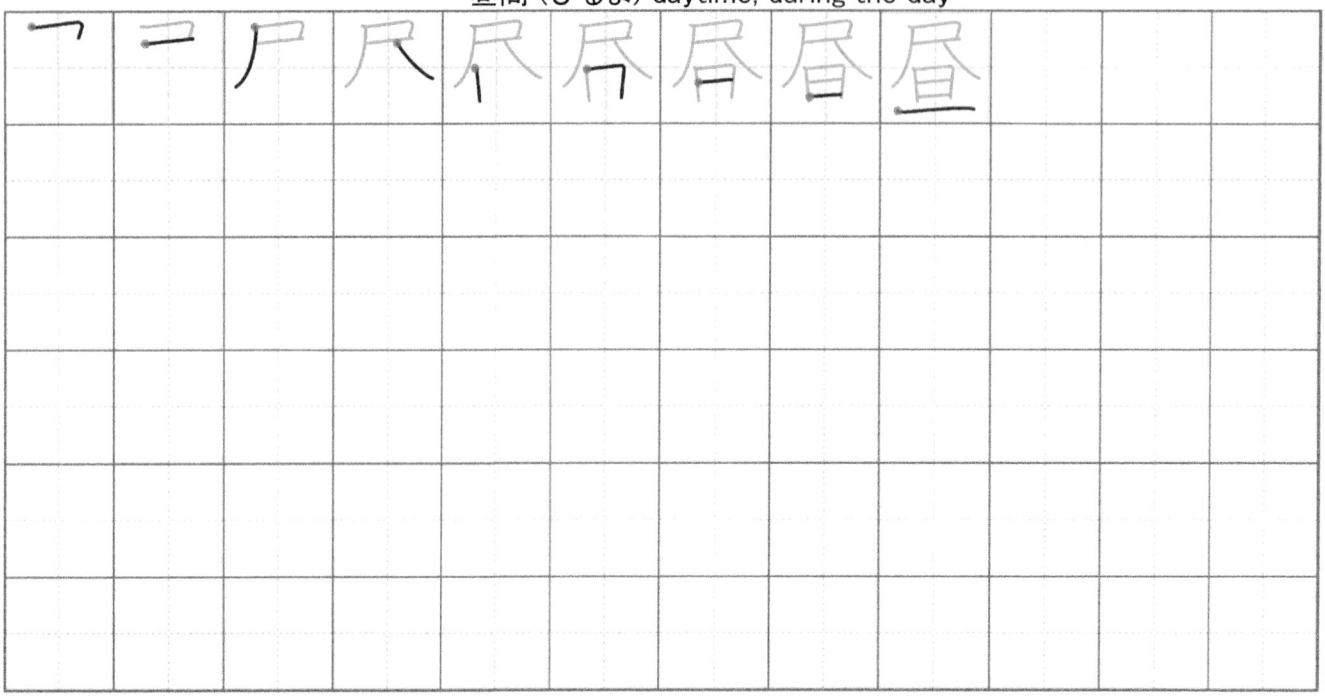

昼

daytime; noon

onyomi チュウ
kunyomi ひる
compounds 昼 (ひる) noon
昼休み (ひるやすみ) lunch (noon) break;
昼御飯 (ひるごはん) lunch
昼間 (ひるま) daytime; during the day

hot; sultry

onyomi　ショ
kunyomi　あつ・い
compounds　暑い（あつい）hot (weather, etc.); warm

い	ﾌ	曱	日	早	早	星	昇	昇	暑	暑	暑

darkness; grow dark

onyomi　アン
kunyomi　くら・い、くら・む、くれ・る
compounds　暗い（くらい）dark; gloomy

l	刀	日	日	日`	日ㅗ	日亠	日立	暗	暗	暗	暗
暗											

曜

onyomi　ヨウ
kunyomi
compounds　土曜日 (どようび) Saturday
　　　　　　日曜日 (にちようび) Sunday
　　　　　　月曜日 (げつようび) Monday

有

exist; happen; possess

onyomi　ユウ
kunyomi　あ・る
compounds　有名 (ゆうめい) famous

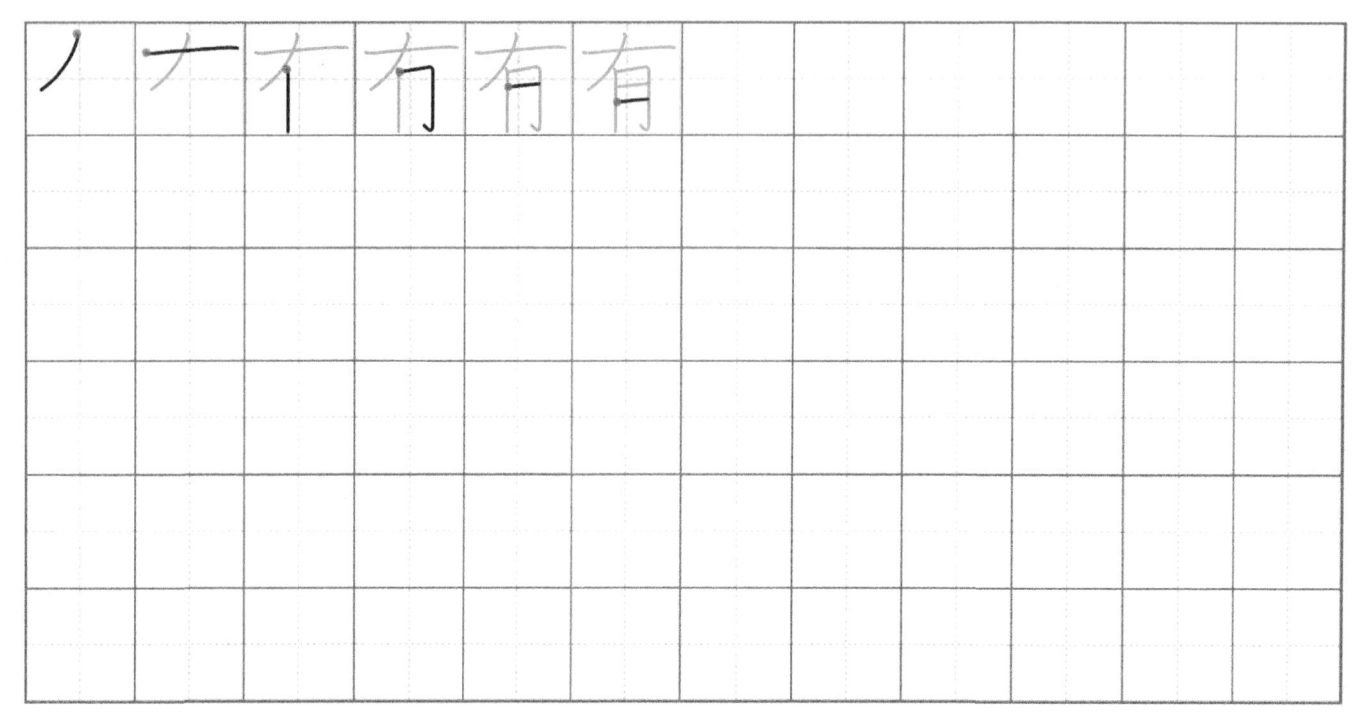

服

onyomi	フク
kunyomi	
compounds	服 (ふく) clothes
	洋服 (ようふく) Western-style clothes

丿	刀	月	月	肝	肛	服	服				

朝

morning; dynasty; period

onyomi	チョウ
kunyomi	あさ
compounds	今朝 (けさ) this morning
	朝 (あさ) morning
	朝御飯 (あさごはん) breakfast
	毎朝 (まいあさ) every morning

一	十	亠	内	吉	吉	亘	卓	卓	朝	朝	朝

town; village

onyomi	ソン
kunyomi	むら
compounds	村 (むら) village

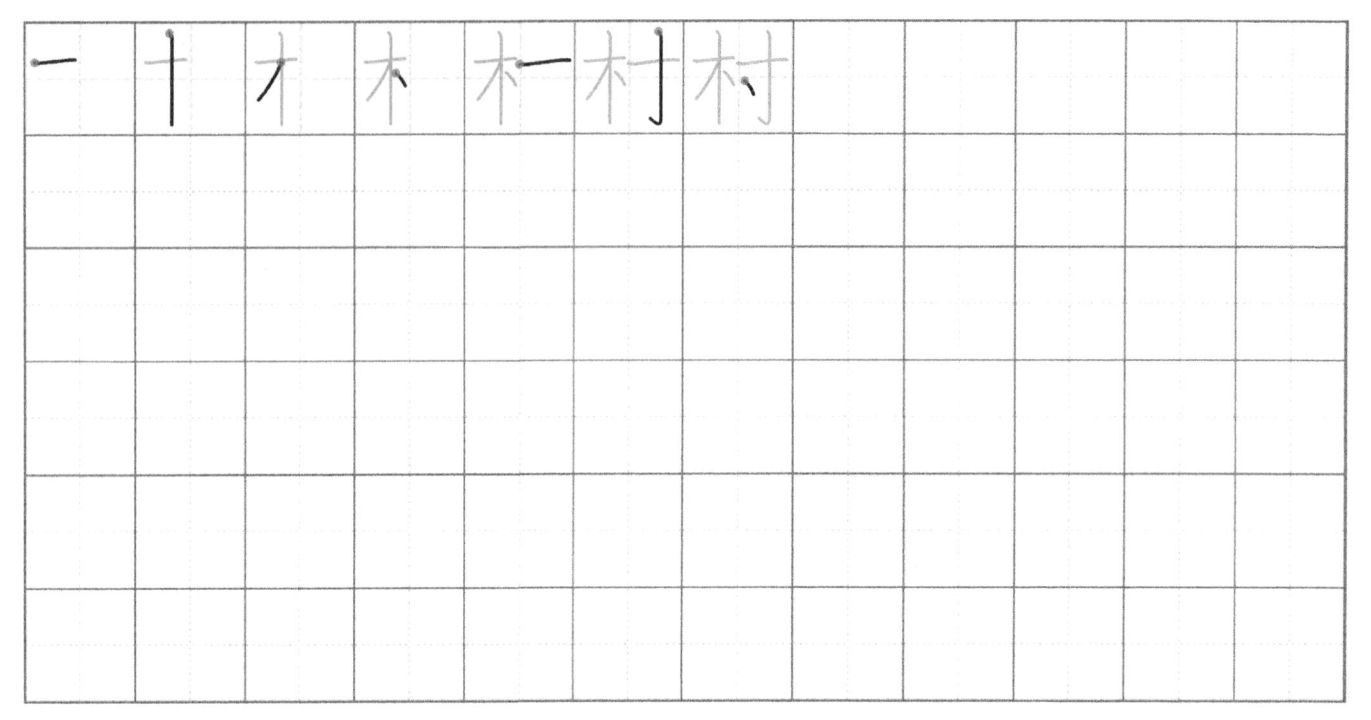

forest; grove

onyomi	リン
kunyomi	はやし
compounds	林 (はやし) woods; thicket

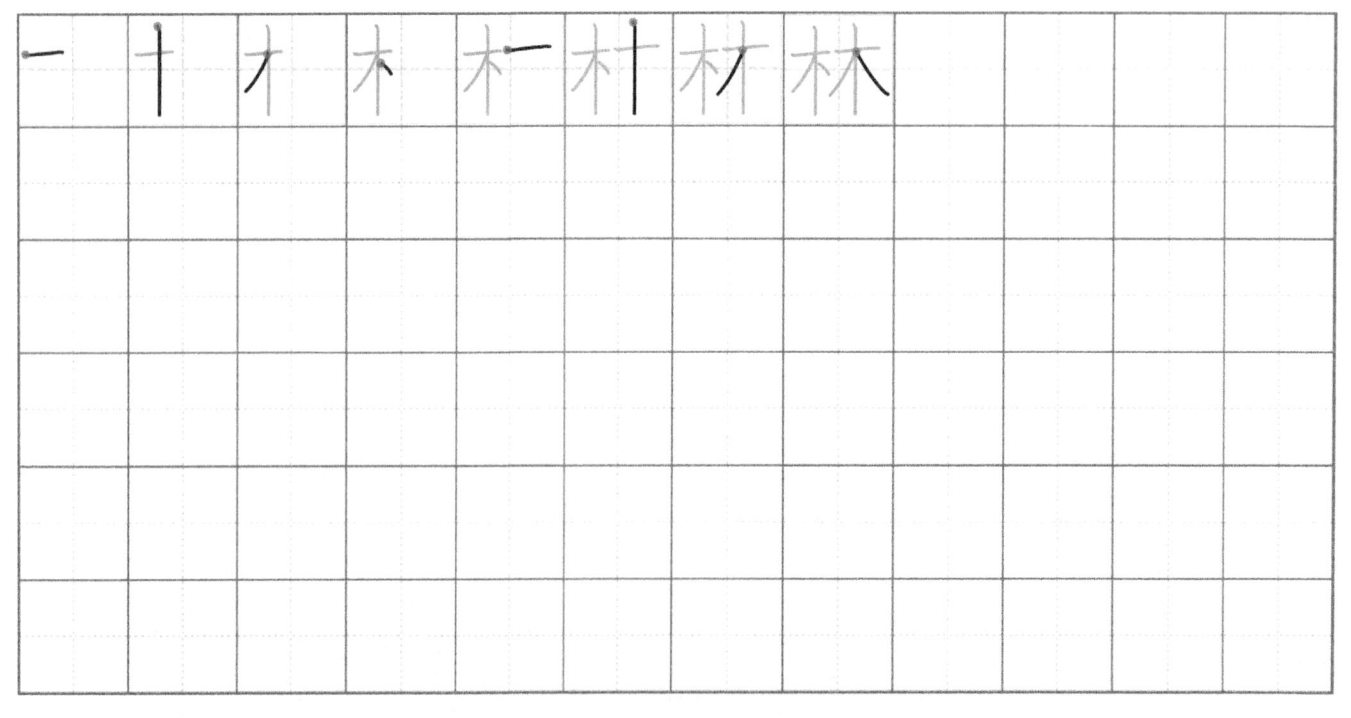

村、林

forest; woods

onyomi	シン
kunyomi	もり
compounds	森 (もり) forest

arts; vocation

onyomi	ギョウ、ゴウ
kunyomi	わざ
compounds	卒業 (そつぎょう) graduation
	工業 (こうぎょう) industry; industrial
	授業 (じゅぎょう) lesson; class work
	産業 (さんぎょう) industry

楽

onyomi	ガク、ゴウ、ラク
kunyomi	この・む、たの・しい、たの・しむ
compounds	楽しい（たのしい）enjoyable; fun
	楽しみ（たのしみ）enjoyment; pleasure
	楽しむ（たのしむ）to enjoy oneself; to have fun
	音楽（おんがく）music

歌

sing; song

onyomi	カ
kunyomi	うた、うた・う
compounds	歌（うた）song
	歌う（うたう）to sing | to recite a poem

止

onyomi シ

kunyomi とど・まる、とど・める、と・まる、と・める、や・む、や・める

compounds 止まる（とまる）to stop
止む（やむ）to cease; to stop
止める（とめる）to stop; to turn off; to park
止める（やめる）to stop (an activity); to quit

正

correct

onyomi ショウ、セイ

kunyomi ただ・しい、まさ・に

compounds 正しい（ただしい）right; correct
正月（しょうがつ）New Year (esp. the first few days); January

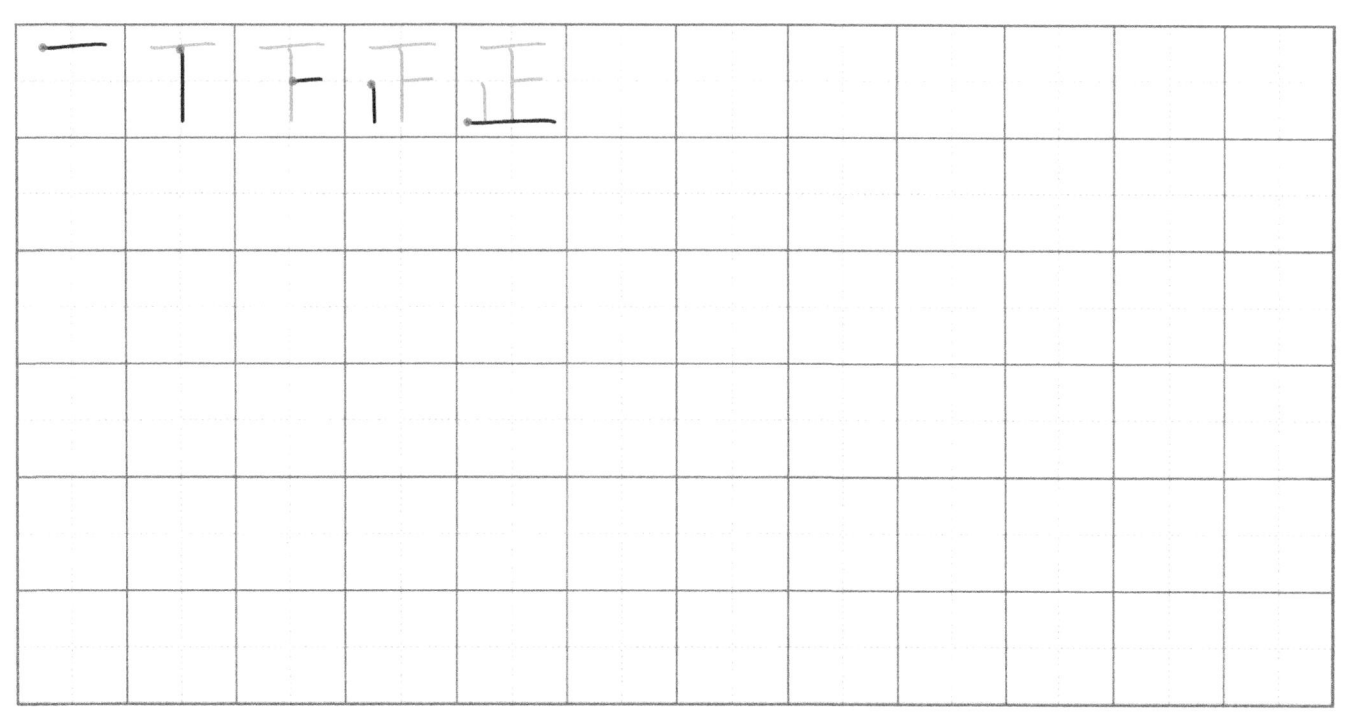

歩

counter for steps; walk

onyomi	フ、ブ、ホ
kunyomi	あゆ・む、ある・く
compounds	散歩 (さんぽ) walk; stroll
	歩く (あるく) to walk

死

death

onyomi	シ
kunyomi	し・ぬ
compounds	死ぬ (しぬ) to die; to pass away

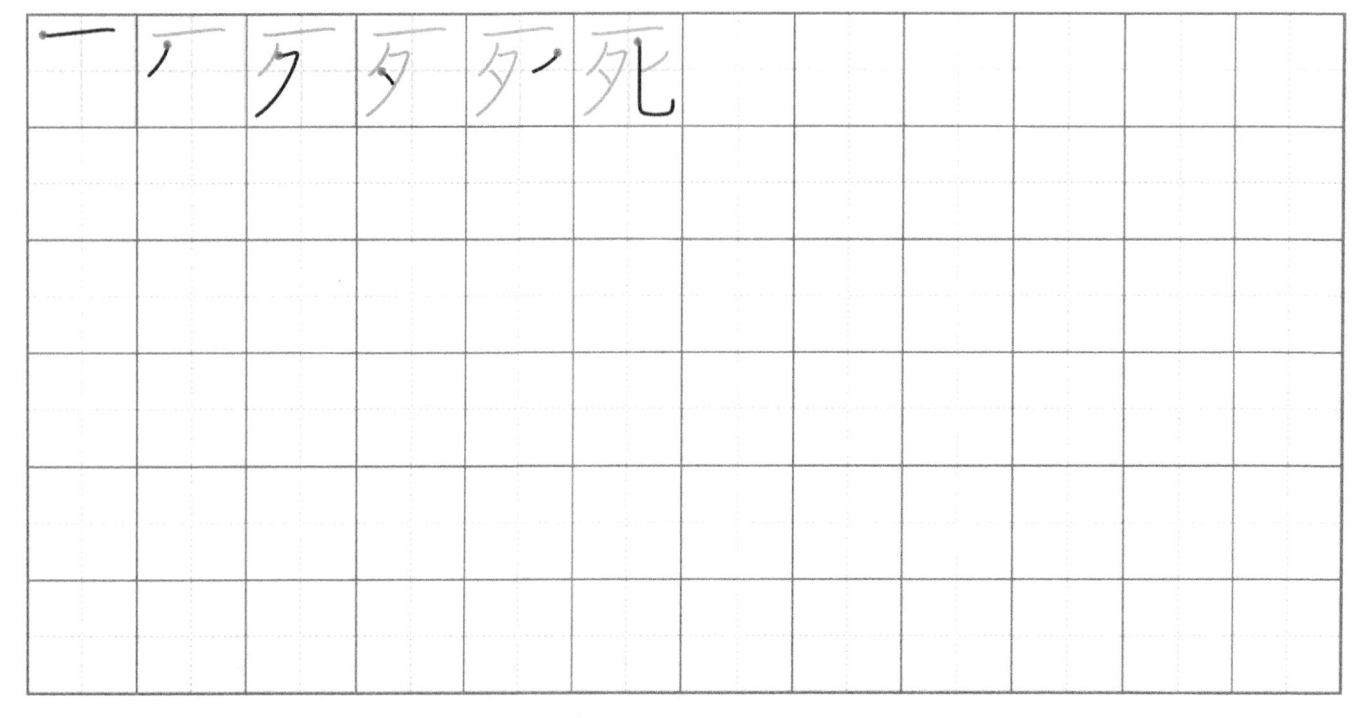

nation; people

onyomi　ミン
kunyomi　たみ
compounds　市民 (しみん) city resident; townspeople

pond; pool

onyomi　チ
kunyomi　いけ
compounds　池 (いけ) pond

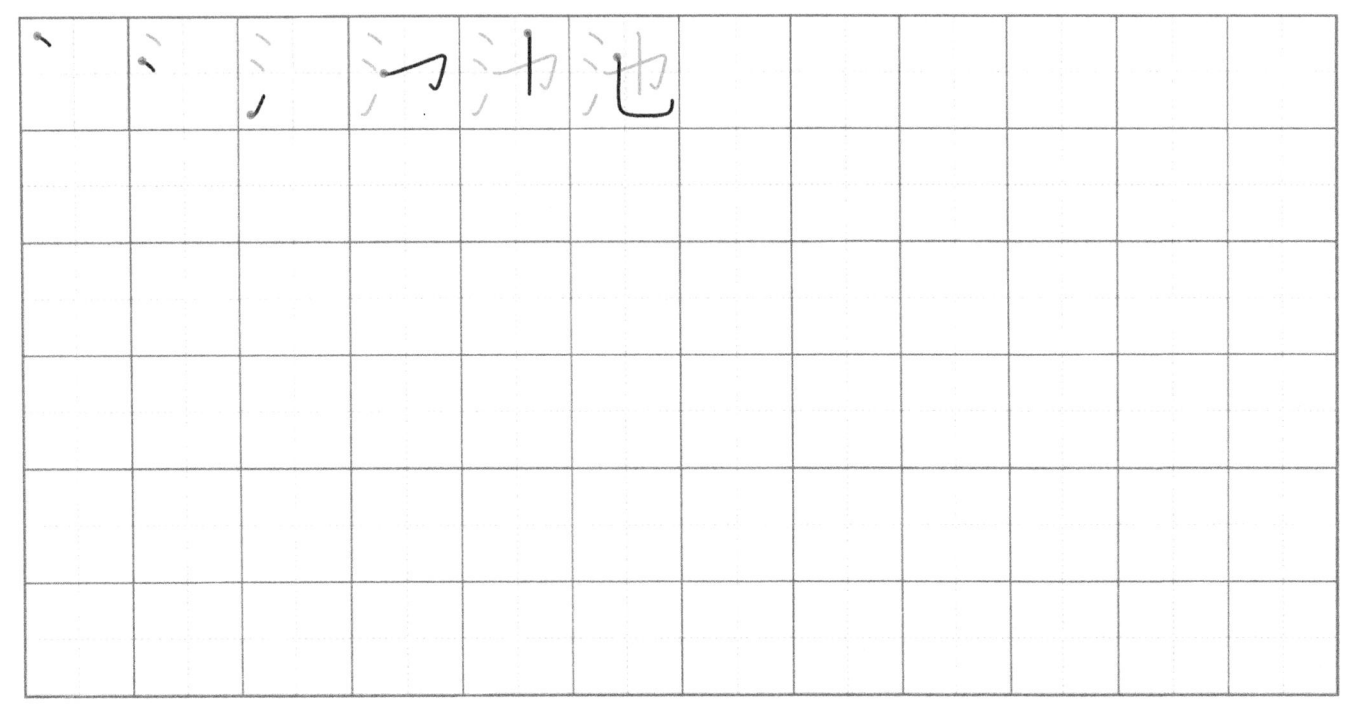

annotate; comment; concentrate on; flow into

onyomi チュウ
kunyomi さ・す、そそ・ぐ、つ・ぐ
compounds 注射（ちゅうしゃ）injection; shot
注意（ちゅうい）caution; attention; warning

ocean; sea; Western style; foreign

onyomi ヨウ
kunyomi
compounds 洋服（ようふく）Western-style clothes
西洋（せいよう）the west; Western countries

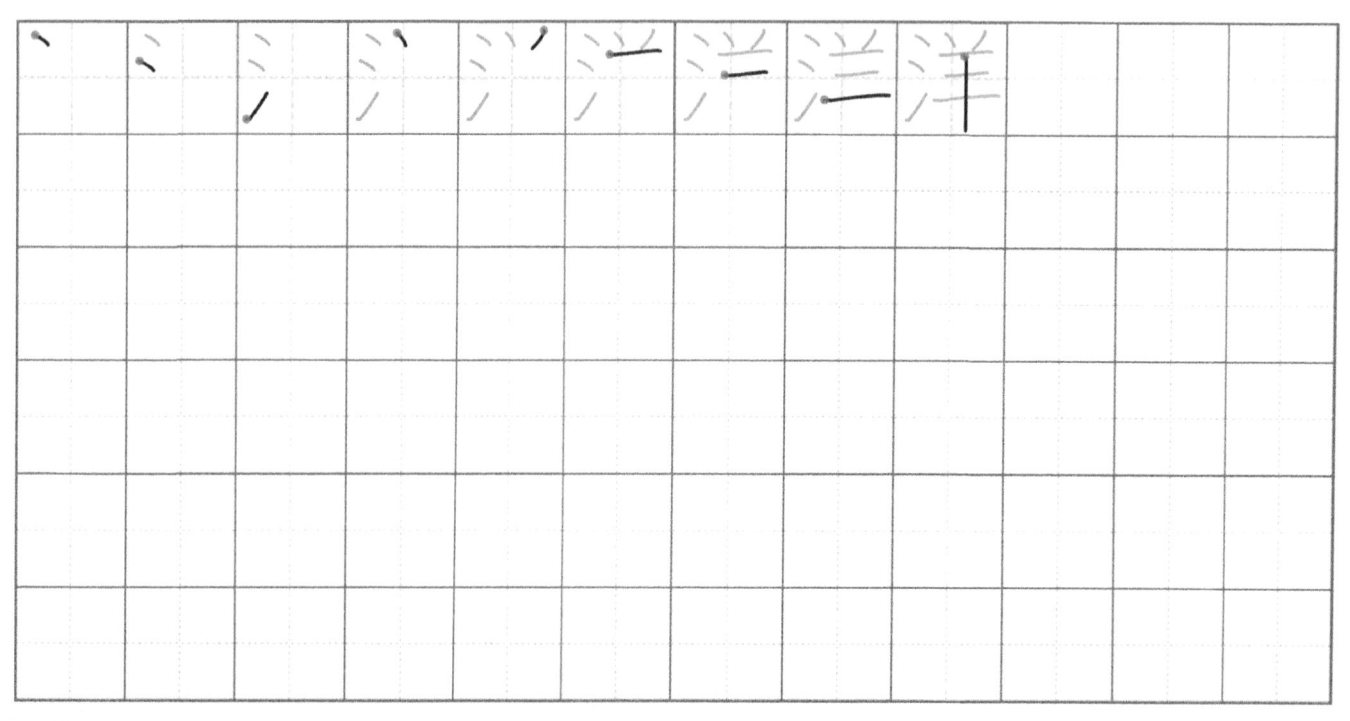

注、洋

inquire into; probe; wash

onyomi	セン
kunyomi	あら・う
compounds	お手洗い（おてあらい）toilet; restroom
	洗う（あらう）to wash; to cleanse
	洗濯（せんたく）washing; laundry

ocean

onyomi	カイ
kunyomi	うみ
compounds	海（うみ）sea; ocean
	海岸（かいがん）coast; beach

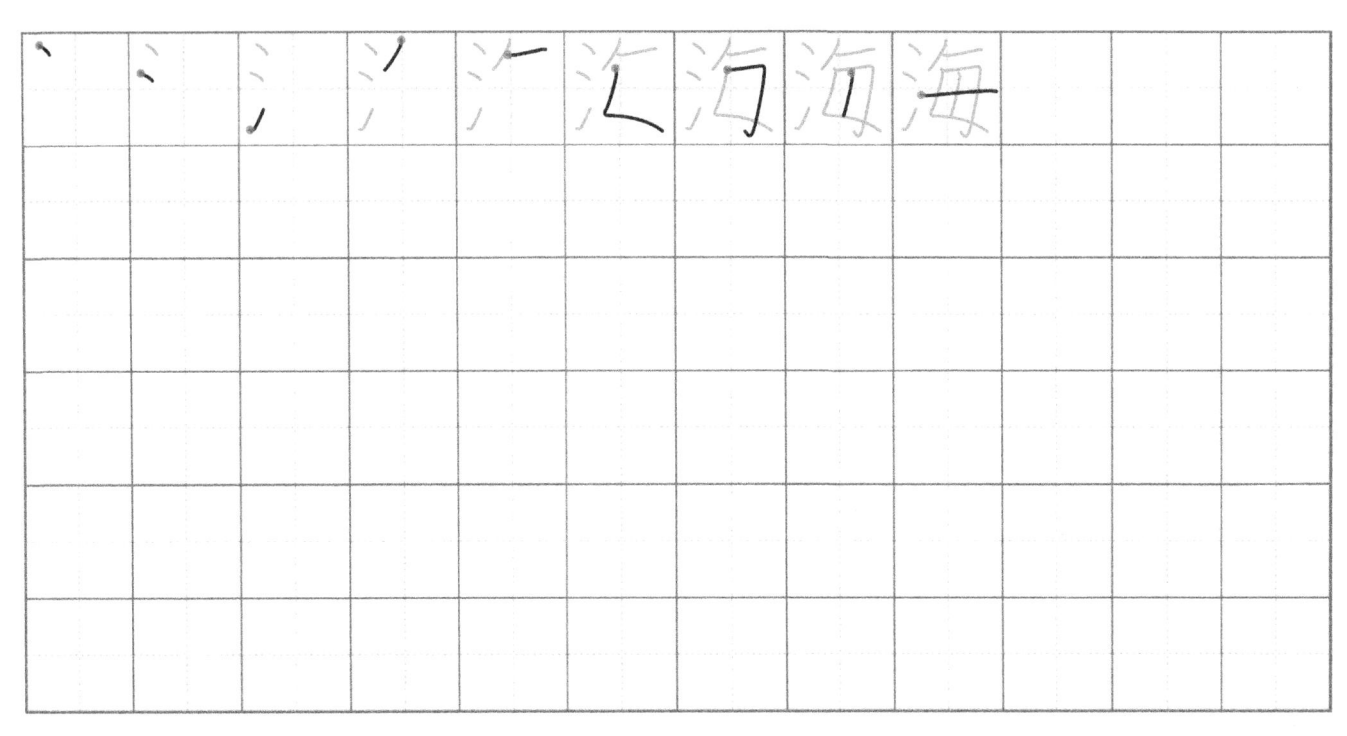

漢

onyomi カン
kunyomi
compounds 漢字 (かんじ) Chinese characters; kanji

丶 シ シ 氵 汁 汁 汗 洪 洪 漢 漢
漢

牛

COW

onyomi ギュウ
kunyomi うし
compounds 牛乳 (ぎゅうにゅう) (cow's) milk
牛肉 (ぎゅうにく) beef

丿 ㇁ 午 牛

物

matter; object; thing

onyomi	ブツ、モツ
kunyomi	もの
compounds	動物 (どうぶつ) animal
	果物 (くだもの) fruit
	荷物 (にもつ) luggage; package
	見物 (けんぶつ) sightseeing; watching

特

special

onyomi	トク
kunyomi	
compounds	特に (とくに) particularly; especially
	特別 (とくべつ) special
	特急 (とっきゅう) limited express (train, faster than an express)

犬

<u>dog</u>

onyomi　ケン
kunyomi　いぬ
compounds　犬 (いぬ) dog

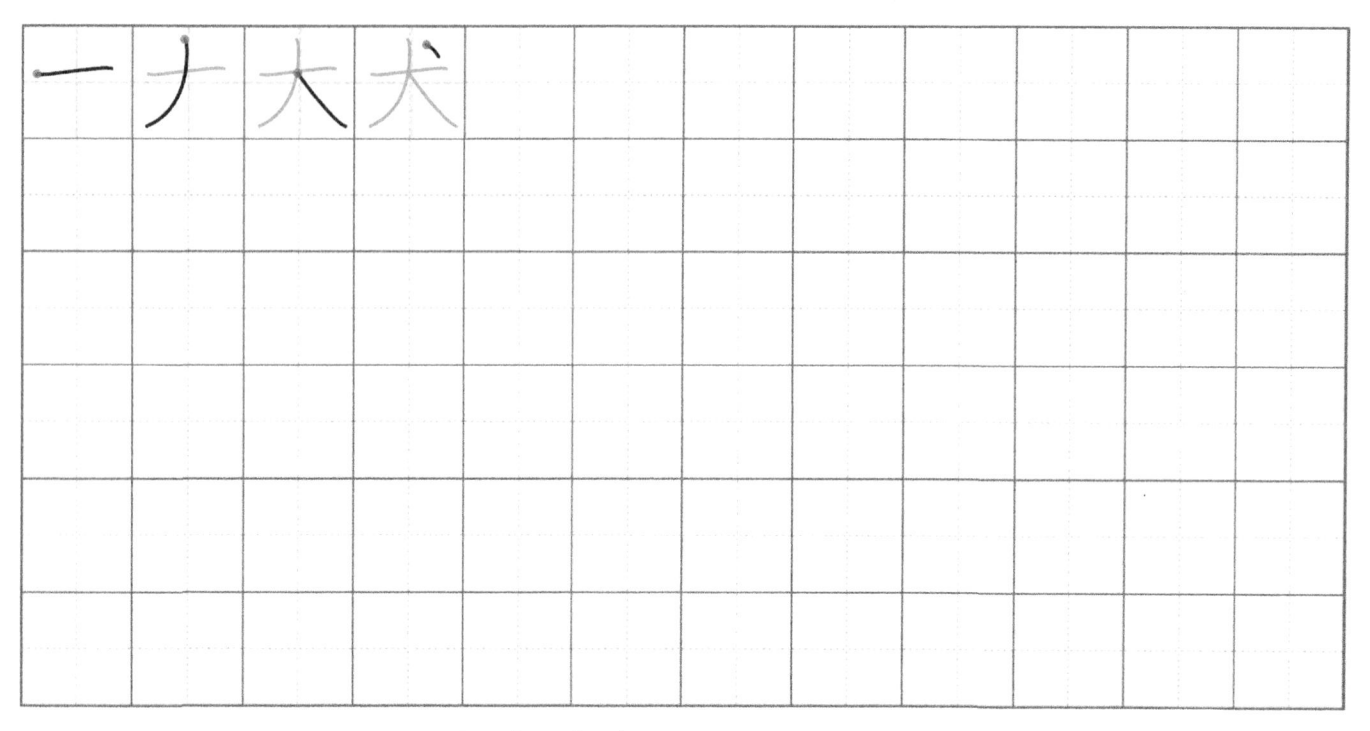

理

arrangement; justice; logic; reason

onyomi　リ
kunyomi　ことわり
compounds　地理 (ちり) geography
　　　　　　料理 (りょうり) cooking; cuisine
　　　　　　無理 (むり) impossible
　　　　　　理由 (りゆう) reason; motive

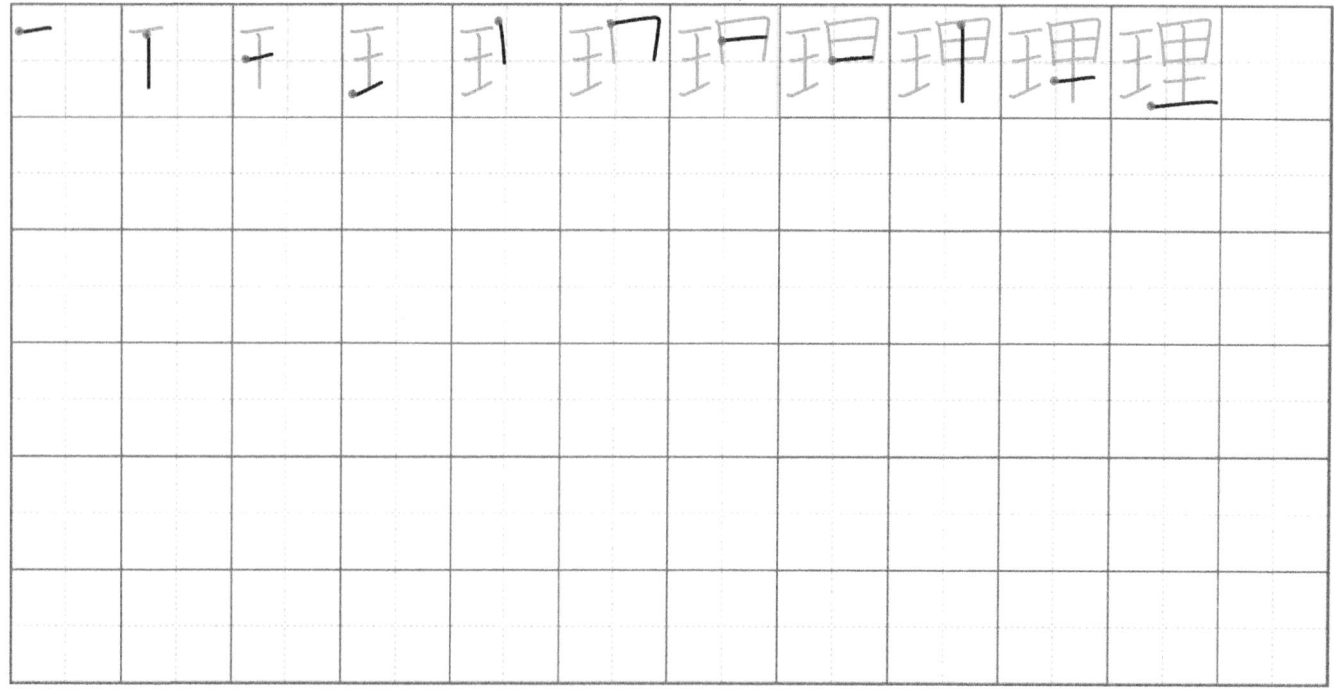

産

childbirth; native; products; property

onyomi	サン
kunyomi	う・まれる、う・む
compounds	お土産 (おみやげ) present; souvenir
	生産 (せいさん) production; manufacture
	産業 (さんぎょう) industry

用

business; employ; use

onyomi	ヨウ
kunyomi	もち・いる
compounds	利用 (りよう) use; utilization
	用 (よう) business; task | use; purpose
	用事 (ようじ) things to do; errand; business (to take care of)
	用意 (ようい) preparation; arrangements

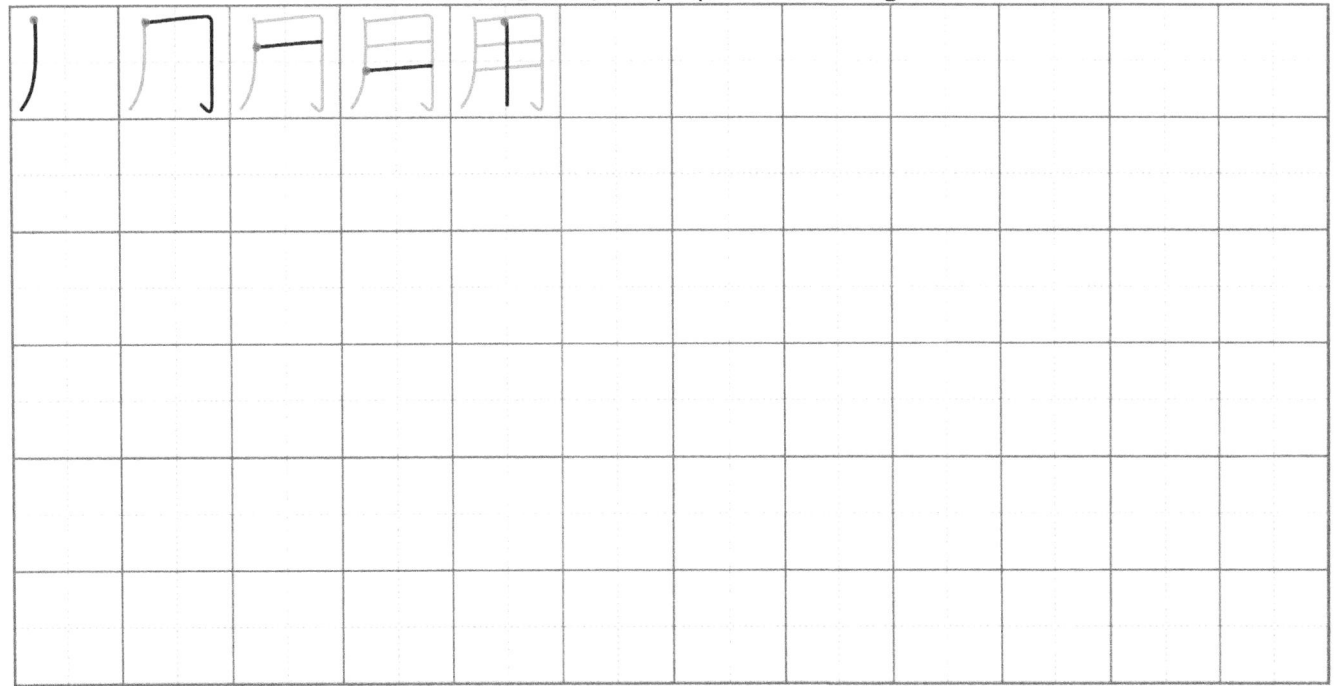

rice field; rice paddy

onyomi デン
kunyomi た
compounds 田舎 (いなか) rural area; countryside

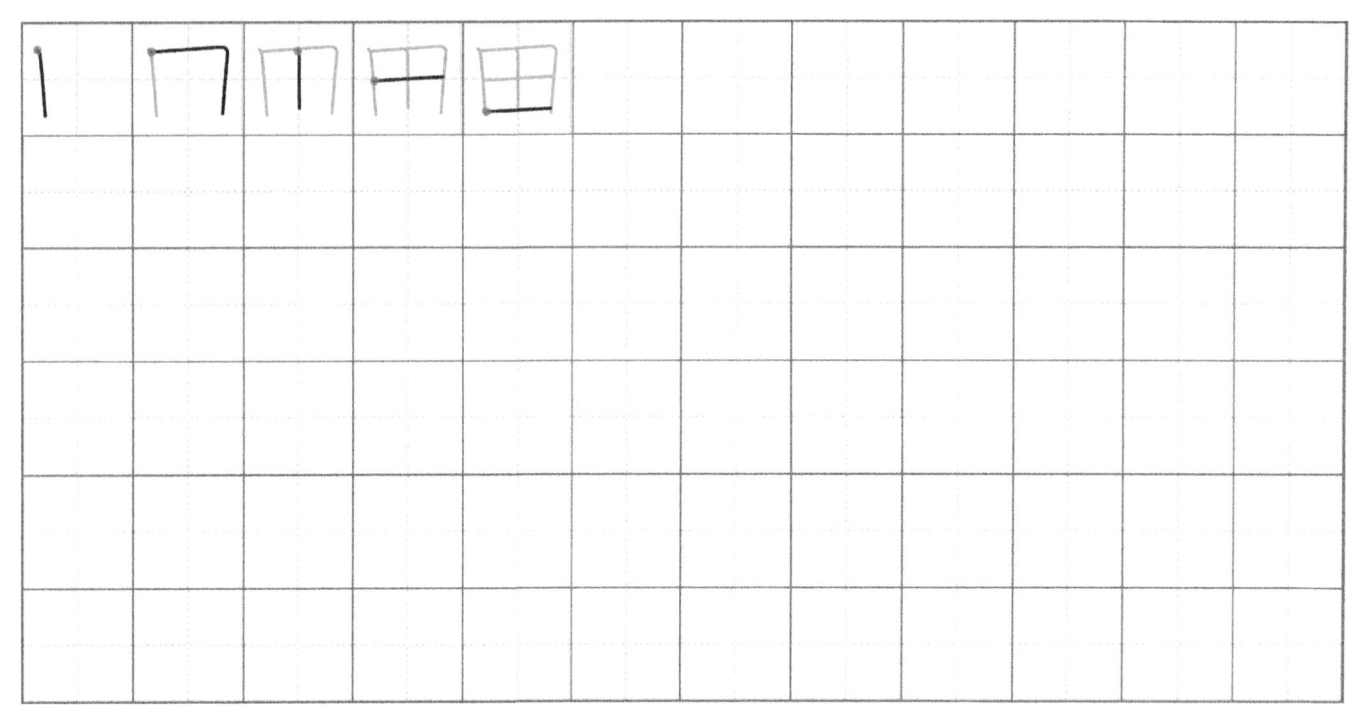

block; street; town; village

onyomi チョウ
kunyomi まち
compounds 町 (まち) town

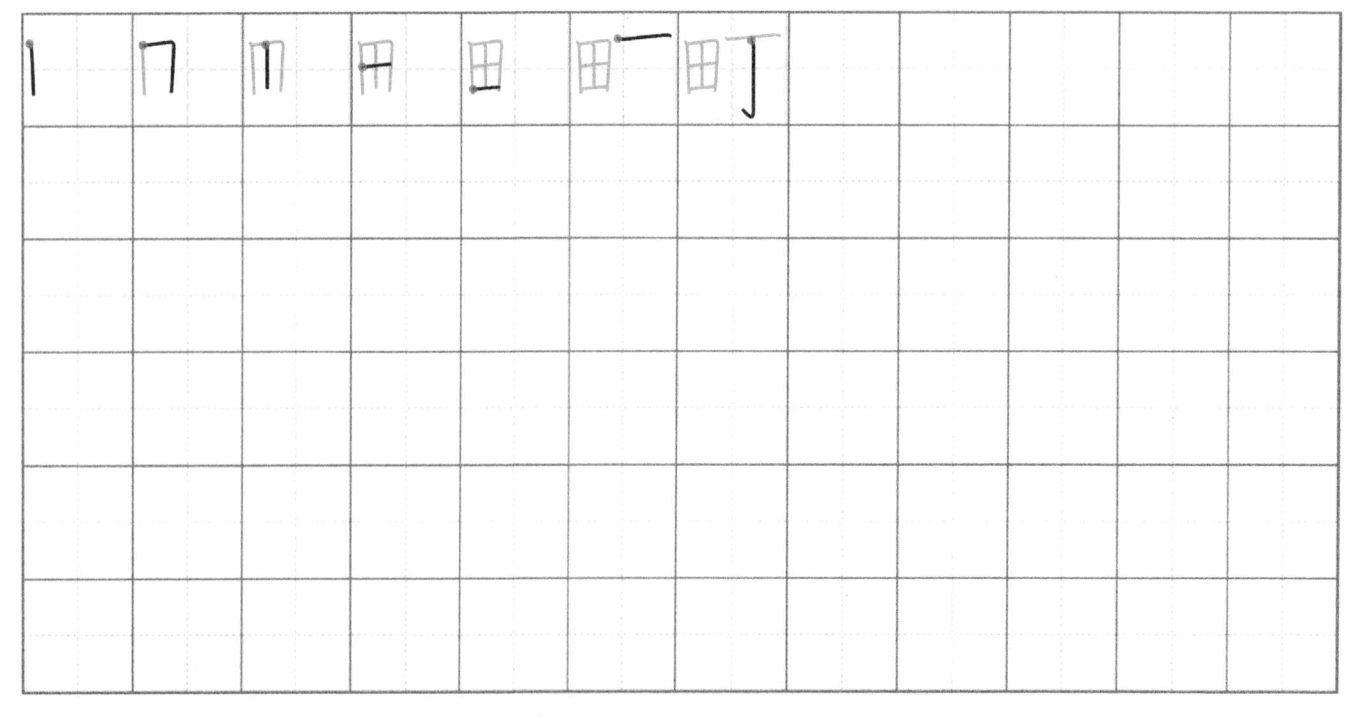

田、町

画

brush-stroke; picture

onyomi エ、カク、ガ
kunyomi えが・く、はか・る
compounds 映画（えいが）movie; film
映画館（えいがかん）movie theatre
漫画（まんが）cartoon; comic
計画（けいかく）plan; schedule

界

boundary; world

onyomi カイ
kunyomi
compounds 世界（せかい）world

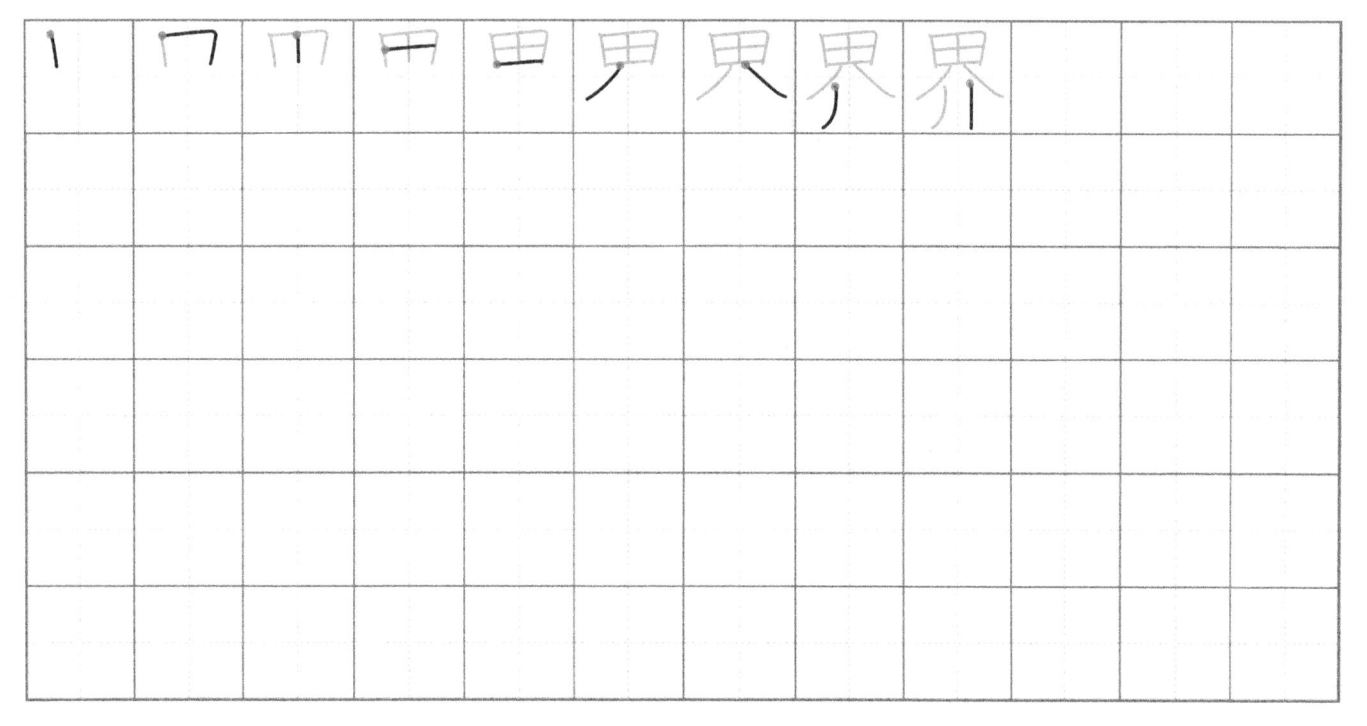

病

ill; sick

onyomi	ビョウ
kunyomi	やまい、や・む
compounds	病気 (びょうき) illness; disease
	病院 (びょういん) hospital

発

departure; disclose; emit; publish; start from

onyomi	ハツ、ホツ
kunyomi	た・つ、つか・わす、はな・つ
compounds	出発 (しゅっぱつ) departure
	発音 (はつおん) pronunciation

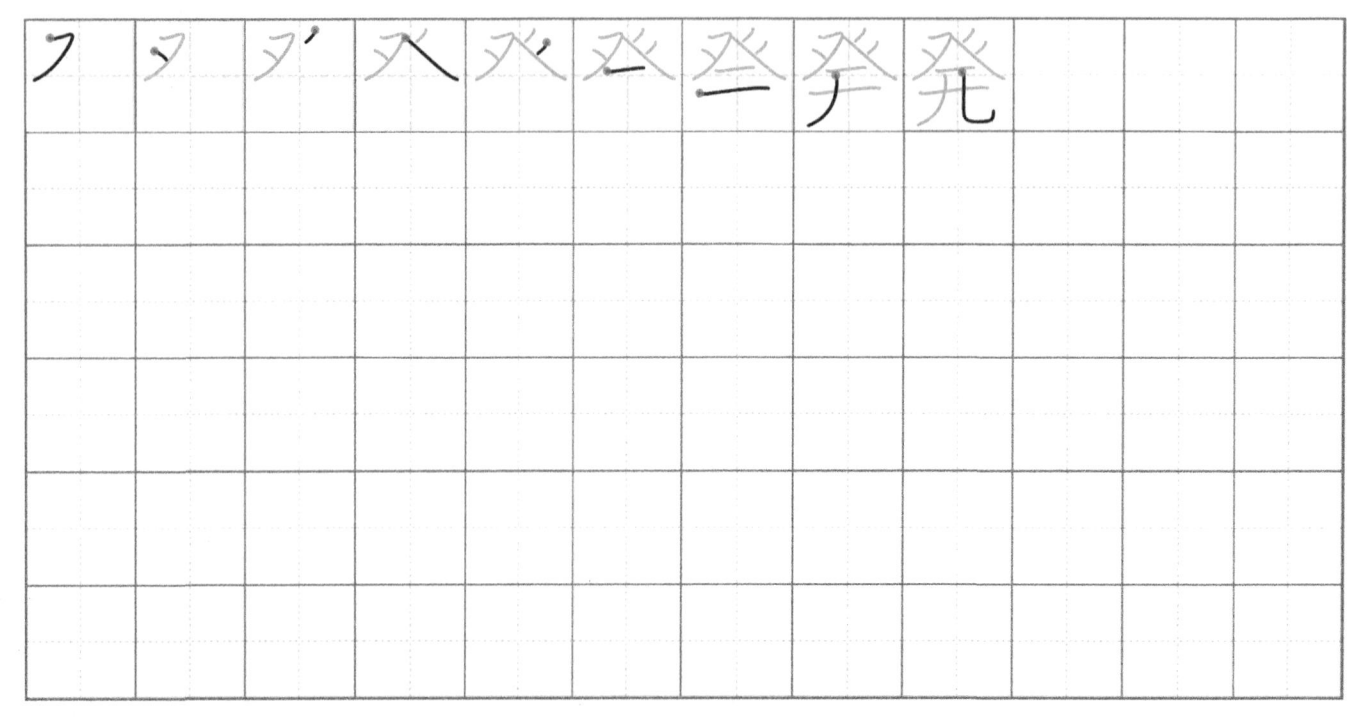

eye; insight; experience; favor

onyomi	ボク、モク
kunyomi	め
compounds	目（め）eye; eyeball
	真面目（まじめ）diligent; serious; honest
	〜目（〜め）number in a sequence

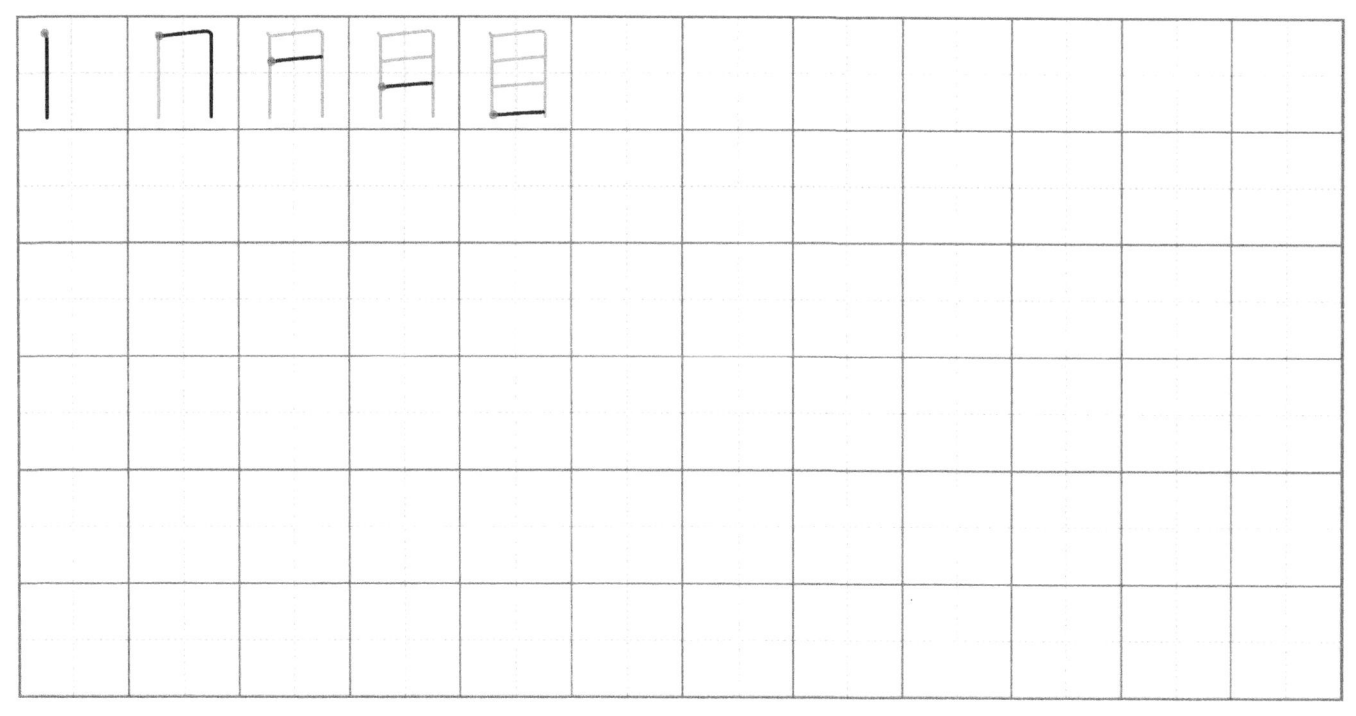

prefecture

onyomi	ケン
kunyomi	
compounds	千葉県（ちばけん）Chiba Prefeture

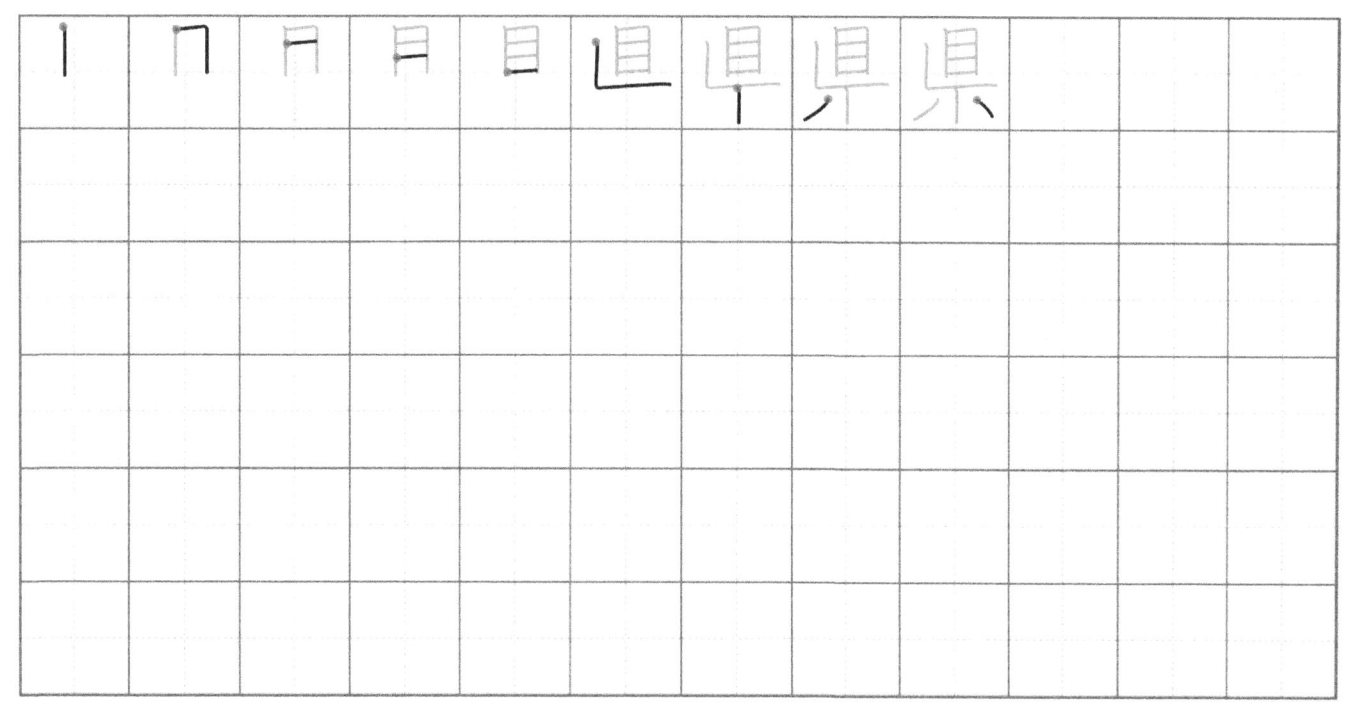

真

Buddhist sect; reality; true

onyomi	シン
kunyomi	ま、まこと
compounds	写真 (しゃしん) photograph; photo; picture
	真中 (まんなか) middle; center
	真面目 (まじめ) diligent; serious; honest

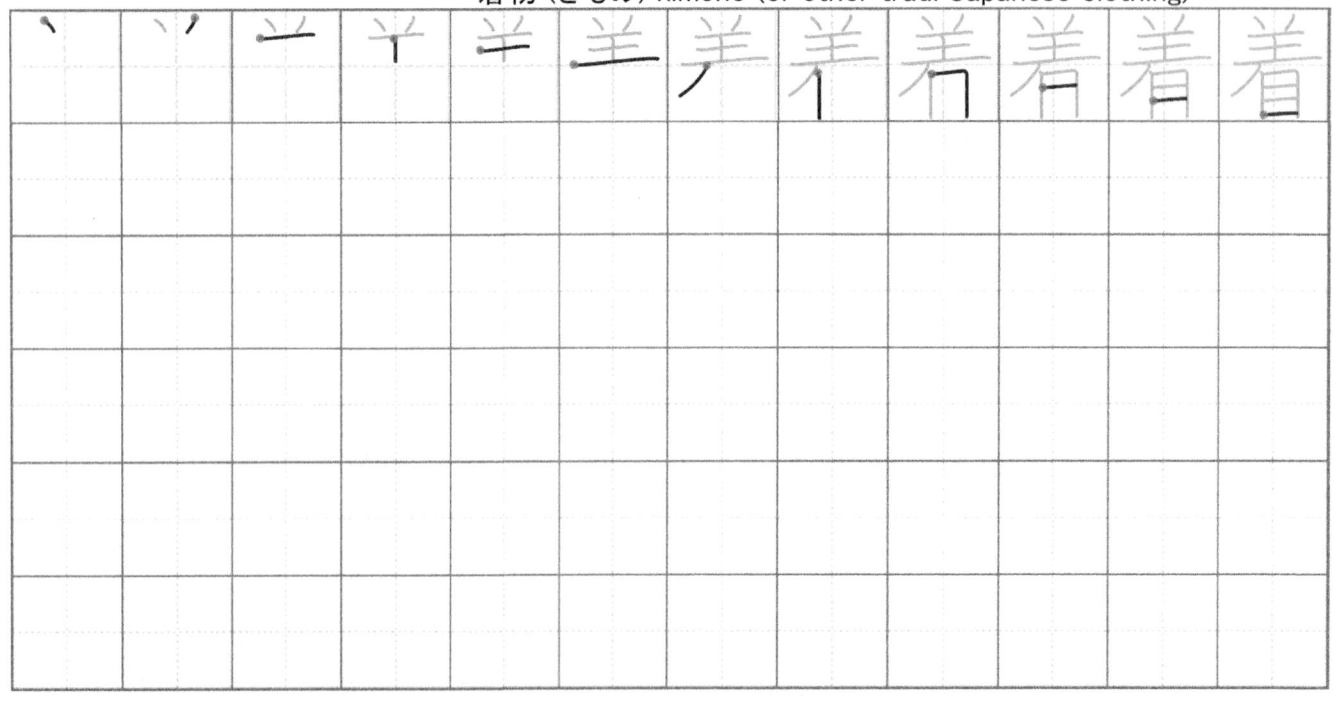

着

arrive; don; wear

onyomi	ジャク、チャク
kunyomi	き・せる、き・る、つ・く、つ・ける
compounds	上着 (うわぎ) coat; tunic; jacket; outer garment
	下着 (したぎ) underwear
	着く (つく) to arrive at; to reach
	着物 (きもの) kimono (or other trad. Japanese clothing)

知

know; wisdom

onyomi	チ
kunyomi	し・らせる、し・る
compounds	承知 (しょうち) consent; acceptance
	知らせる (しらせる) to notify; to inform
	知る (しる) to know

ノ	⻑	⻗	矢	矢	矢	知	知			

短

brevity; short; defect; fault

onyomi	タン
kunyomi	みじか・い
compounds	短い (みじかい) short

ノ	⻑	⻗	矢	矢	矢	知	知	知	知	短	短

研

polish; sharpen

onyomi	ケン
kunyomi	と・ぐ
compounds	研究 (けんきゅう) study; research
	研究室 (けんきゅうしつ) laboratory

社

association; company; shrine

onyomi	シャ
kunyomi	やしろ
compounds	会社 (かいしゃ) company
	社会 (しゃかい) society
	社長 (しゃちょう) company president
	神社 (じんじゃ) Shinto shrine

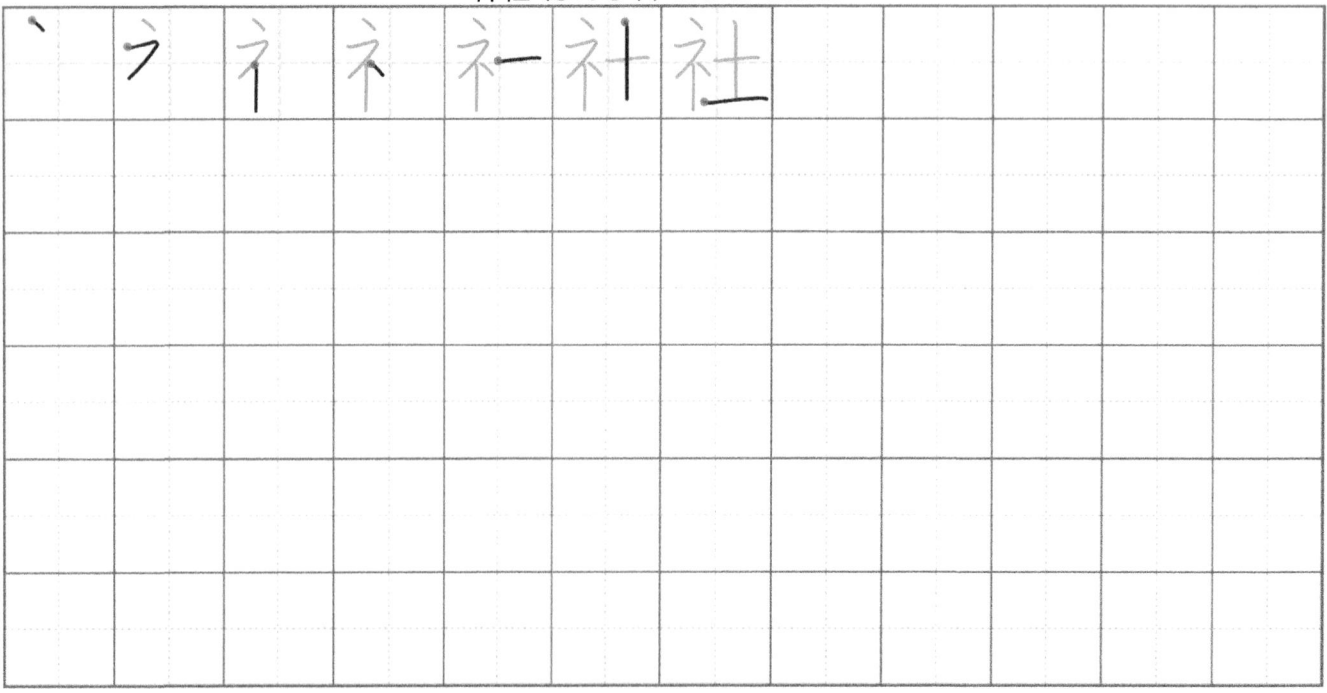

私

I; me; private

onyomi	シ
kunyomi	わたくし、わたし
compounds	私（わたし）I; me

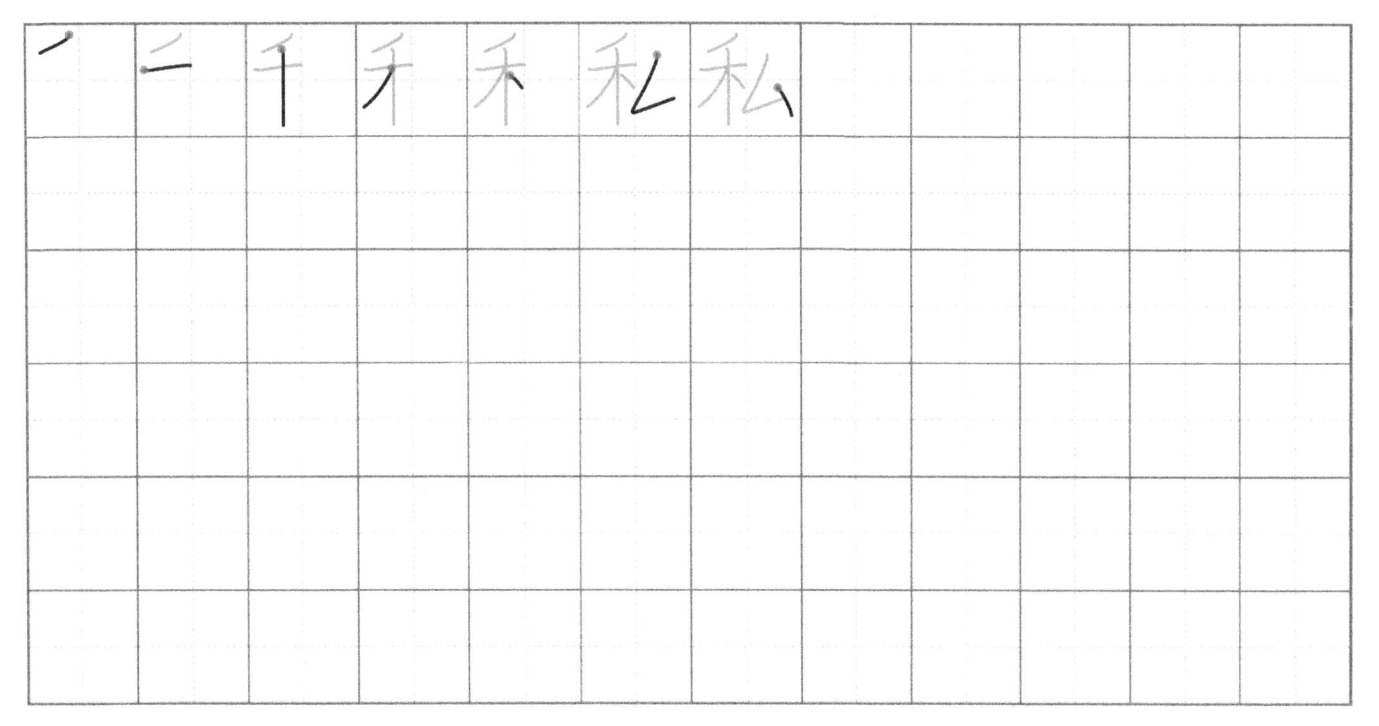

秋

autumn

onyomi	シュウ
kunyomi	あき
compounds	秋（あき）autumn; fall

究

research; study

onyomi キュウ、ク
kunyomi きわ・める
compounds 研究 (けんきゅう) study; research
研究室 (けんきゅうしつ) laboratory

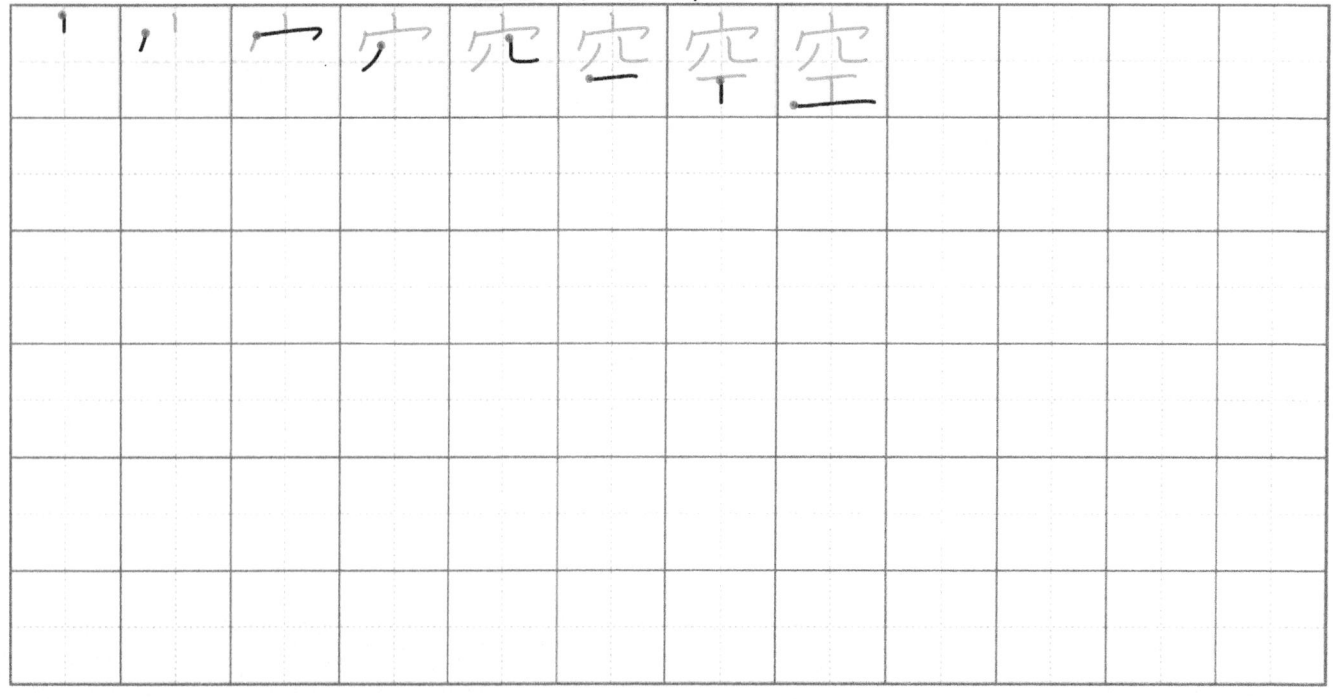

空

empty; vacuum; sky

onyomi クウ
kunyomi あ・く、あ・ける、から、す・く
compounds 空く (あく) (あく) to be open; to become empty
空く (すく) (すく) to become less crowded; to get empty
空気 (くうき) air; atmosphere | mood; situation
空港 (くうこう) airport

立

erect; rise; stand up

onyomi	リツ、リュウ
kunyomi	た・つ、た・てる
compounds	役に立つ (やくにたつ) to be useful
	立つ (たつ) to stand; to rise
	立てる (たてる) to stand up; to erect
	立派 (りっぱ) splendid; fine

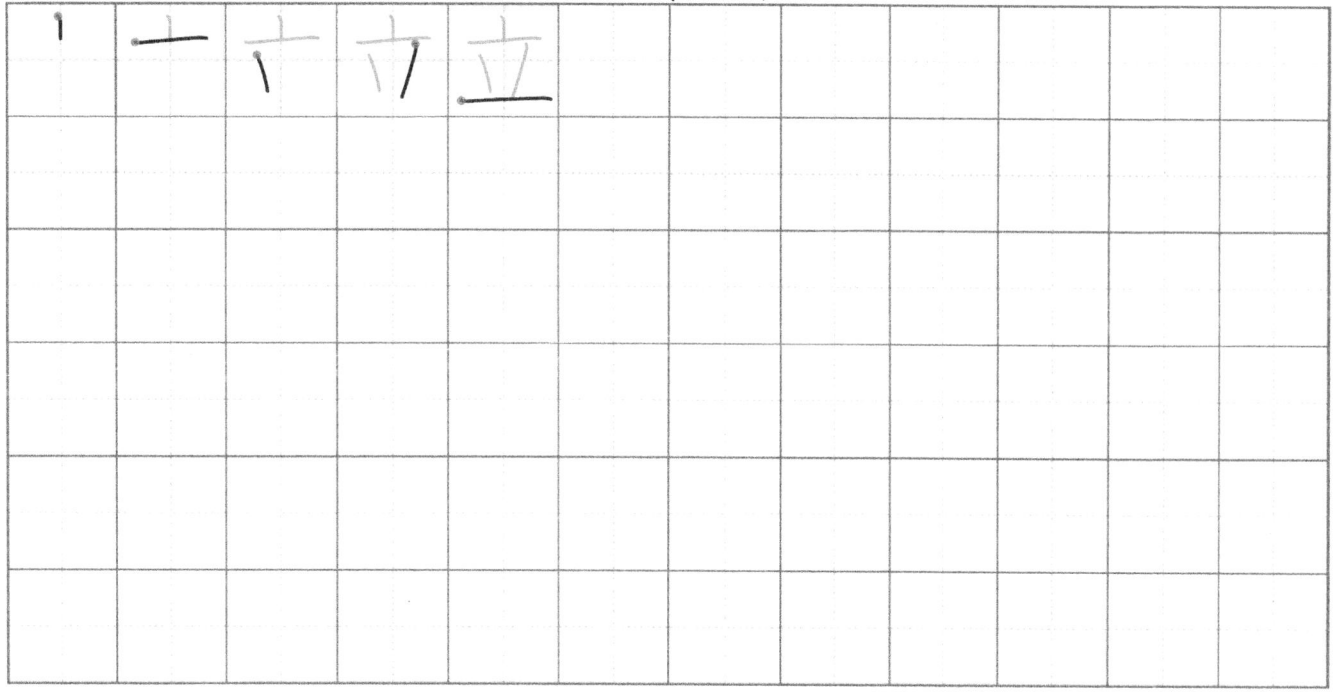

答

answer; solution

onyomi	トウ
kunyomi	こた・える
compounds	答 (こたえ) answer; reply
	答える (こたえる) to answer; to reply

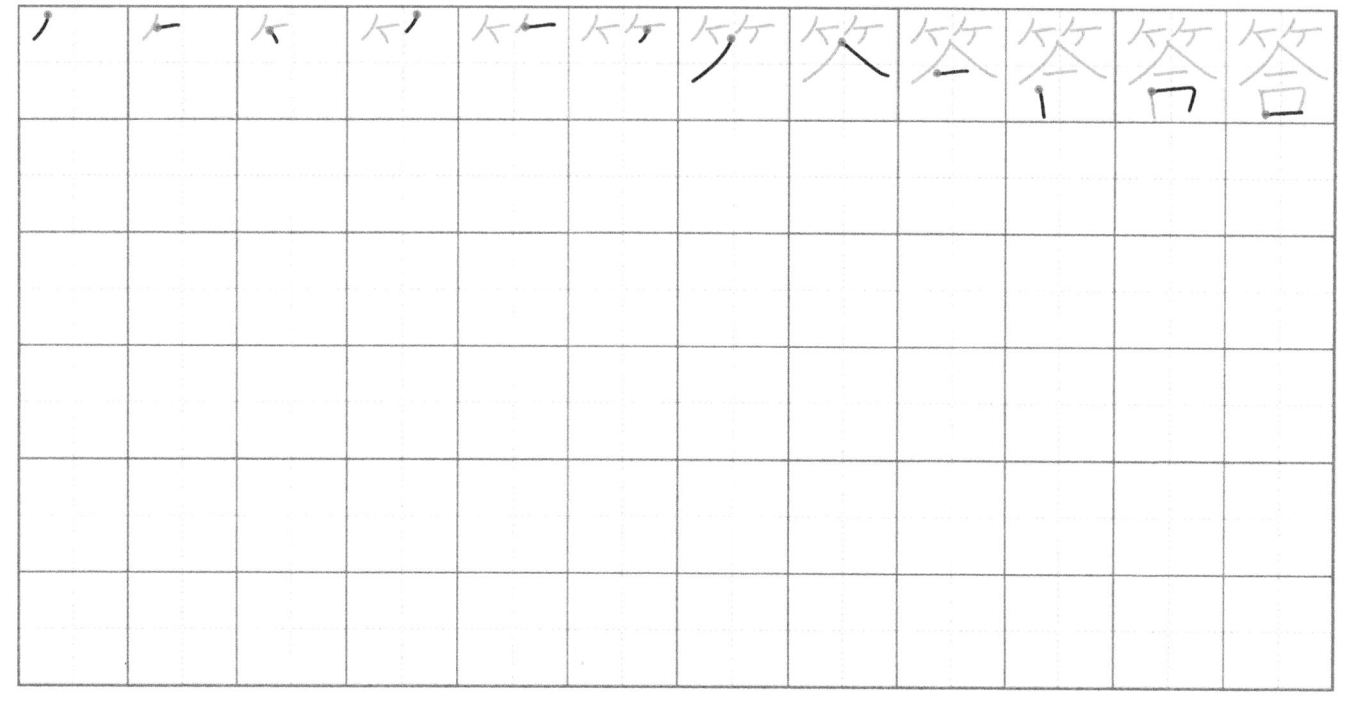

紙

paper

onyomi	シ
kunyomi	かみ
compounds	手紙 (てがみ) letter
	紙 (かみ) paper

終

end; finish

onyomi	シュウ
kunyomi	お・える、お・わる
compounds	終わり (おわり) the end
	終わる (おわる) to end; to finish

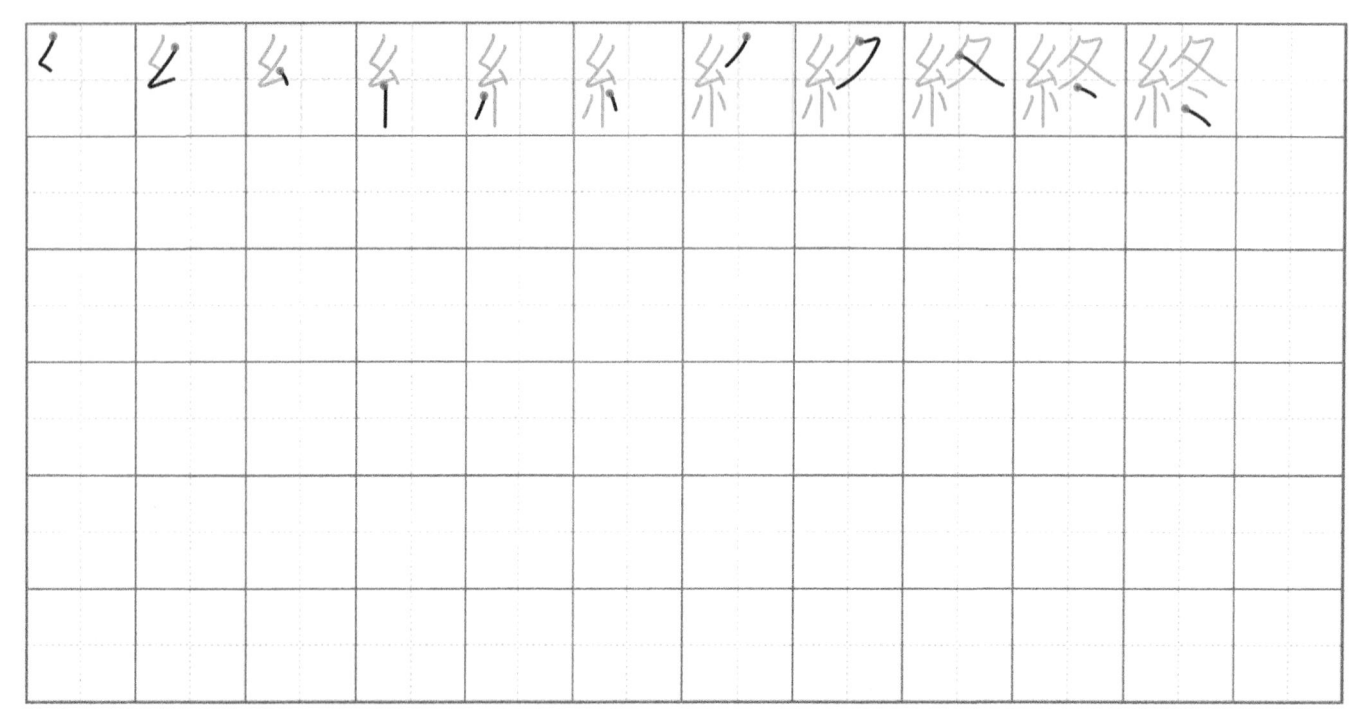

learn

onyomi	シュウ
kunyomi	なら・う
compounds	予習 (よしゅう) preparation for a lesson
	復習 (ふくしゅう) review
	練習 (れんしゅう) practice
	習慣 (しゅうかん) habit; custom

consider

onyomi	コウ
kunyomi	かんが・える
compounds	考える (かんがえる) to think; to ponder

者

onyomi	シャ
kunyomi	もの
compounds	医者 (いしゃ) doctor
	歯医者 (はいしゃ) dentist

一　十　土　耂　者　者　者　者

肉

meat

onyomi	ニク
kunyomi	
compounds	牛肉 (ぎゅうにく) beef
	肉 (にく) flesh | meat
	豚肉 (ぶたにく) pork
	鶏肉 (とりにく) chicken meat

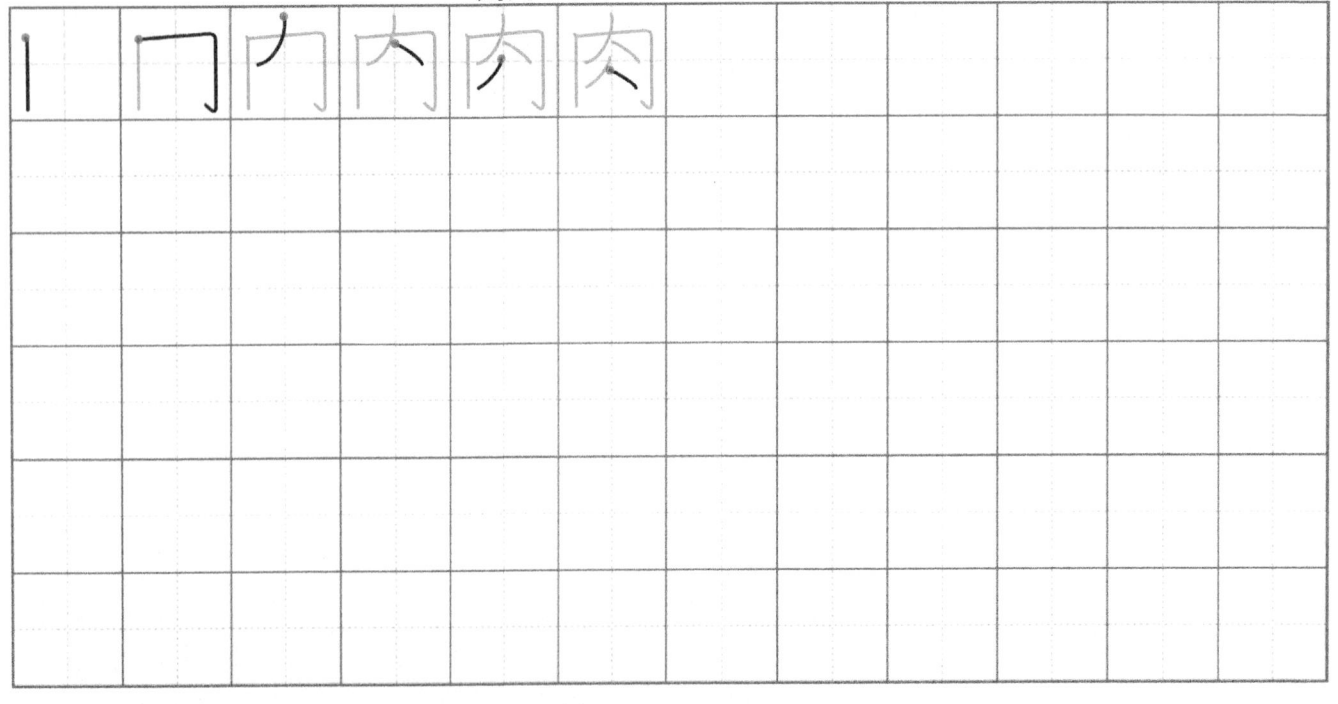

者、肉

oneself

onyomi	シ、ジ	
kunyomi	みずか・ら	
compounds	自分 (じぶん) myself; oneself	
	自動車 (じどうしゃ) automobile	
	自由 (じゆう) freedom	
	自転車 (じてんしゃ) bicycle	

color

onyomi	シキ、ショク	
kunyomi	いろ	
compounds	景色 (けしき) scenery; scene; landscape	
	色々 (いろいろ) various	
	茶色 (ちゃいろ) brown	
	黄色い (きいろい) yellow	

花

flower

onyomi カ
kunyomi はな
compounds 花 (はな) flower
花瓶 (かびん) (flower) vase
花見 (はなみ) cherry blossom viewing

英

England; English

onyomi エイ
kunyomi
compounds 英語 (えいご) English

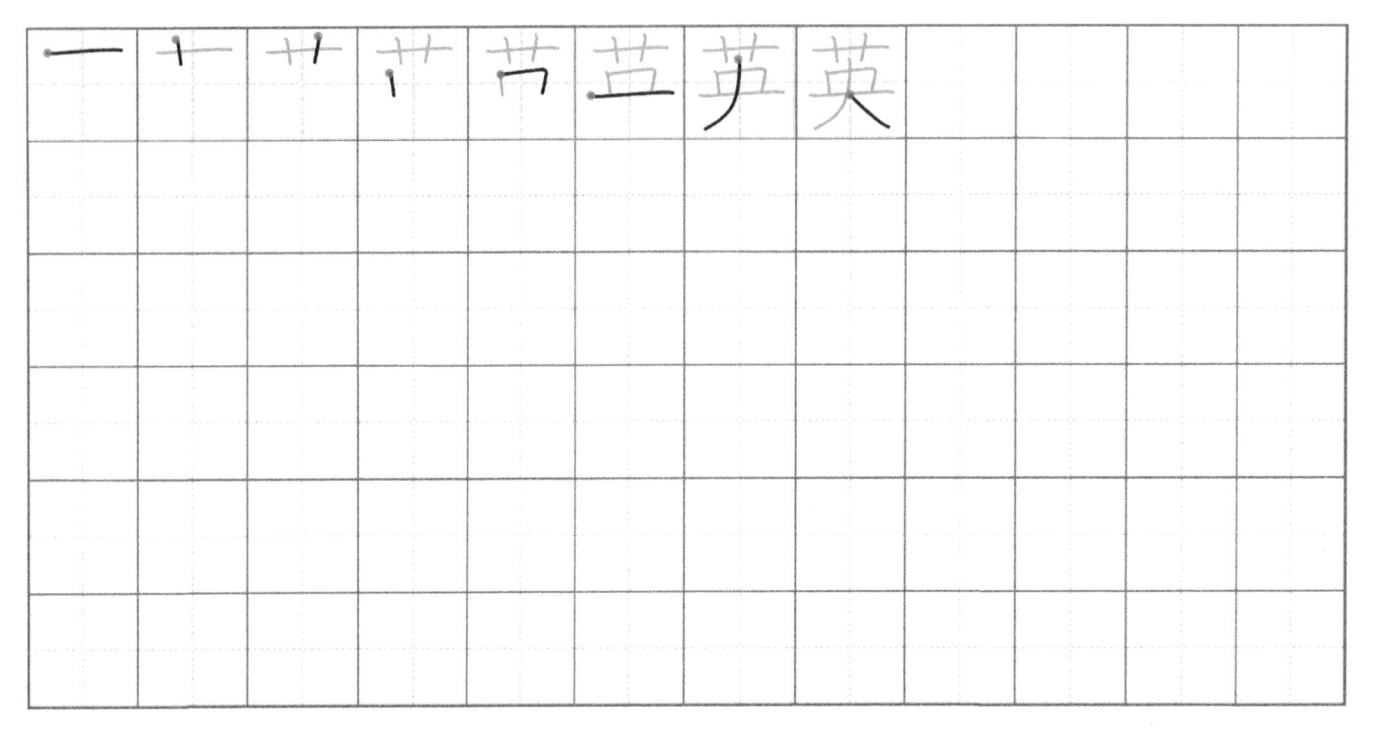

tea

onyomi	サ、チャ
kunyomi	
compounds	お茶 (おちゃ) tea (usu. Green)
	喫茶店 (きっさてん) coffee shop; cafe
	紅茶 (こうちゃ) black tea
	茶色 (ちゃいろ) brown

一 十 十 サ サ 芝 芝 茶 茶

greens; vegetable

onyomi	サイ
kunyomi	な
compounds	野菜 (やさい) vegetable

一 十 十 サ サ 芝 芝 苙 苙 菜 菜

薬

chemical; medicine

onyomi ヤク
kunyomi くすり
compounds 薬 (くすり) medicine; pharmaceuticals

一 十 艹 茫 艻 苩 苩 苩 茜 薄 薄
薄 薄 薄 薬

親

parent; relative; intimacy

onyomi シン
kunyomi おや、した・しい、した・しむ
compounds 両親 (りょうしん) both parents
親 (おや) parent(s)
親切 (しんせつ) kindness; gentleness

` 一 宀 立 立 立 辛 亲 亲 新 新 新
新 親 親 親

say; word

onyomi	ゲン、ゴン
kunyomi	い・う
compounds	言う (いう) to say; to utter
	言葉 (ことば) word; phrase

measure; plan

onyomi	ケイ
kunyomi	はか・る
compounds	時計 (とけい) watch; clock
	計画 (けいかく) plan; schedule

試

onyomi シ
kunyomi こころ・みる、ため・す
compounds 試合（しあい）match; game
試験（しけん）exam; test

説

explanation; opinion

onyomi セツ、ゼイ
kunyomi と・く
compounds 小説（しょうせつ）novel; (short) story
説明（せつめい）explanation; exposition

買 <u>buy</u>

onyomi	バイ
kunyomi	か・う
compounds	買い物 (かいもの) shopping; purchased goods
	買う (かう) to buy

貸 <u>lend</u>

onyomi	タイ
kunyomi	か・す
compounds	貸す (かす) to lend

質

onyomi　シチ、シツ、チ

kunyomi

compounds　質問 (しつもん) question; inquiry

赤

red

onyomi　シャク、セキ

kunyomi　あか、あか・い、あか・らむ、あか・らめる

compounds　赤 (あか) red; crimson; scarlet

赤い (あかい) red

赤ちゃん (あかちゃん) baby

赤ん坊 (あかんぼう) baby; infant

走

<u>run</u>

onyomi ソウ
kunyomi はし・る
compounds 走る（はしる）to run

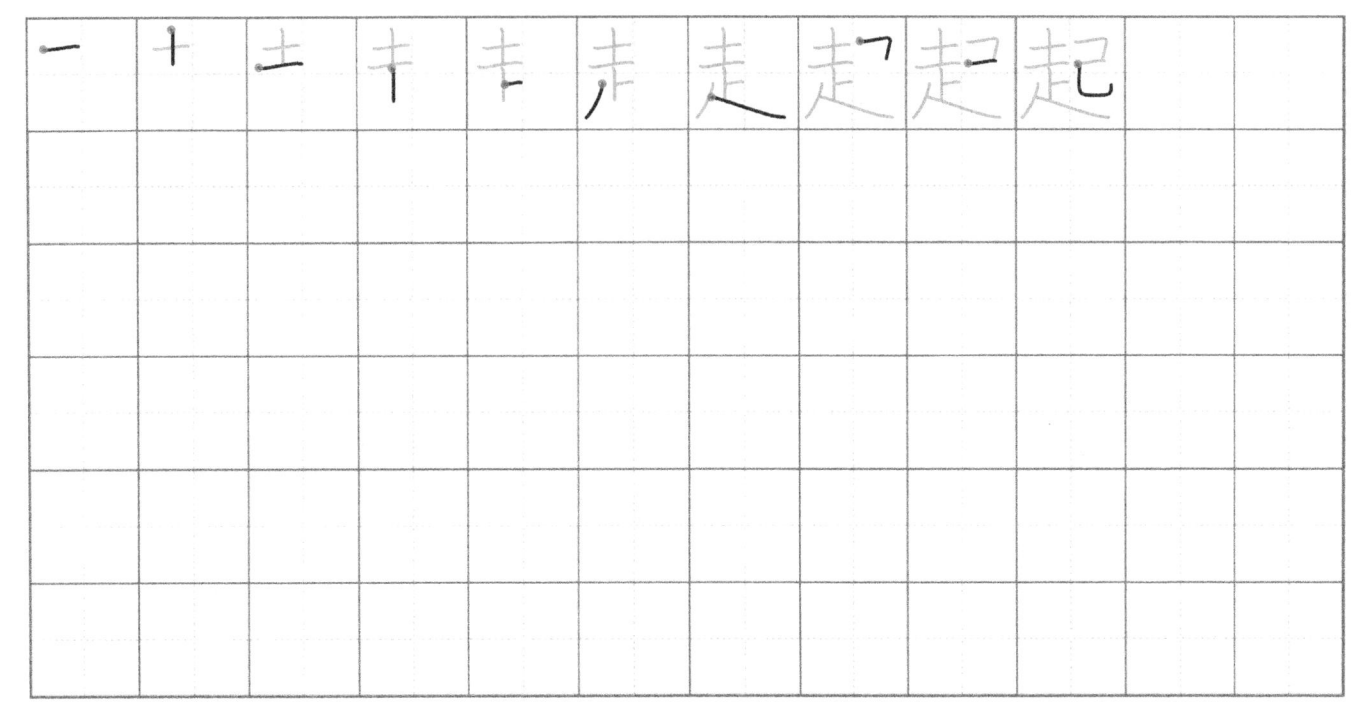

起

<u>get up; wake up</u>

onyomi キ
kunyomi お・きる、お・こす、お・こる
compounds 起きる（おきる）to get up; to wake up
起こす（おこす）to wake up
起す（おこす）to wake up

足

leg; foot; be sufficient

onyomi　ソク

kunyomi　あし、た・す、た・りる、た・る

compounds　足 (あし) foot | leg

足す (たす) to add

足りる (たりる) to be sufficient; to be enough

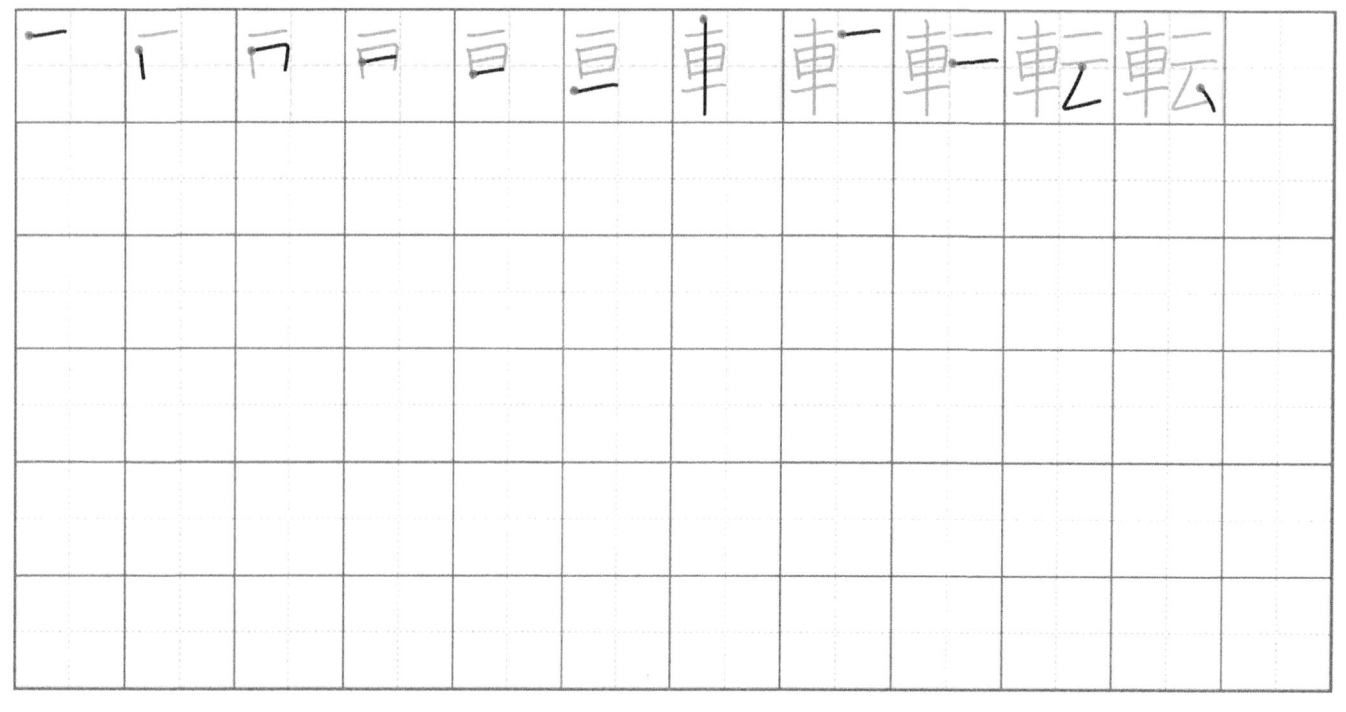

転

revolve

onyomi　テン

kunyomi　ころ・がす、ころ・がる、ころ・げる、ころ・ぶ

compounds　自転車 (じてんしゃ) bicycle

運転 (うんてん) operation (of a machine, etc.); driving

運転手 (うんてんしゅ) driver; chauffeur

軽

onyomi　ケイ
kunyomi　かる・い、かろ・やか
compounds　軽い (かるい) light (i.e. not heavy)

近

akin; near

onyomi　キン、コン
kunyomi　ちか・い
compounds　最近 (さいきん) recently
　　　　　　近い (ちかい) near; close
　　　　　　近く (ちかく) near
　　　　　　近所 (きんじょ) neighborhood

送

escort; send

onyomi	ソウ
kunyomi	おく・る
compounds	放送 (ほうそう) broadcast
	送る (おくる) to send; to dispatch | to escort

通

avenue; commute; pass through

onyomi	ツ、ツウ
kunyomi	かよ・う、とお・す、とお・る
compounds	交通 (こうつう) traffic; transportation; communication
	普通 (ふつう) usual; ordinary
	通う (かよう) to go to (school, work, etc.); to commute
	通り (とおり) street; road

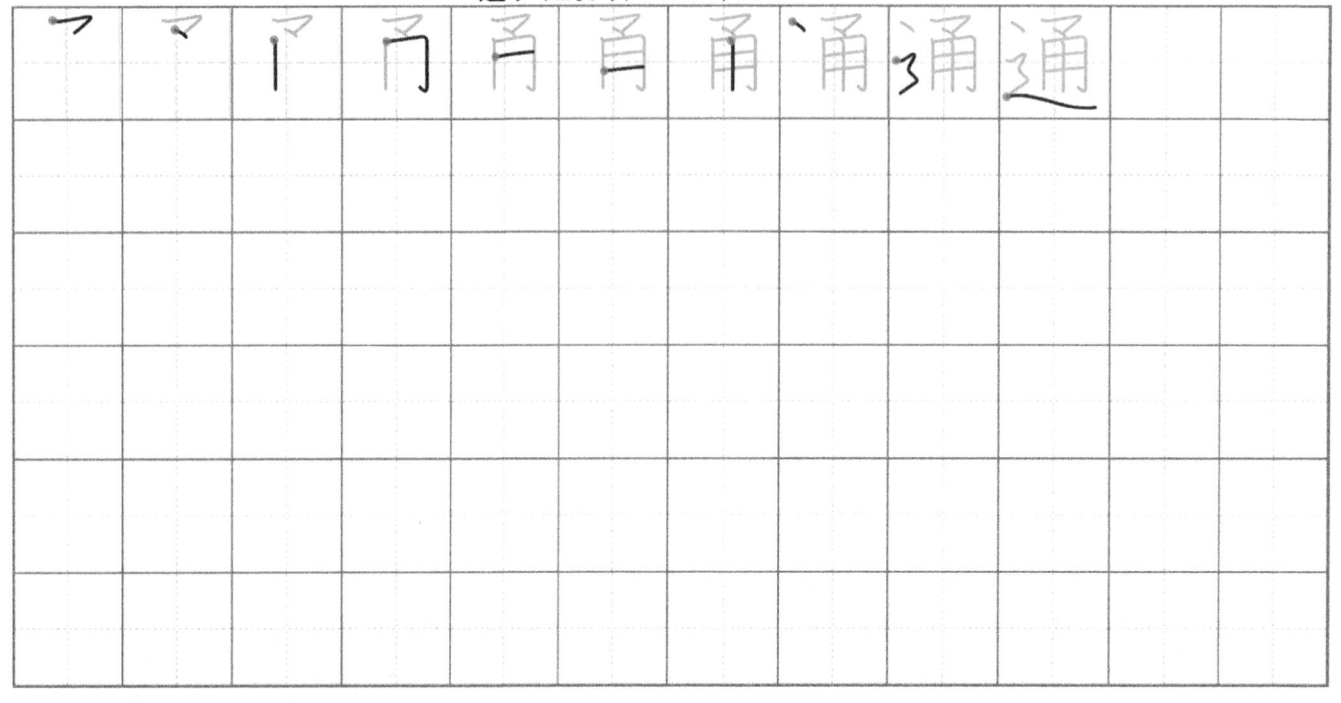

week

onyomi シュウ
kunyomi
compounds 今週（こんしゅう）this week
来週（らいしゅう）next week
毎週（まいしゅう）every week
〜週間（〜しゅうかん）period of weeks

advance; proceed

onyomi シン
kunyomi すす・む、すす・める
compounds 進む（すすむ）to advance; to proceed

運

carry; destiny; fate

onyomi	ウン
kunyomi	はこ・ぶ
compounds	運ぶ (はこぶ) to carry
	運動 (うんどう) exercise; physical training
	運転 (うんてん) operation (of a machine, etc.); driving
	運転手 (うんてんしゅ) driver; chauffeur

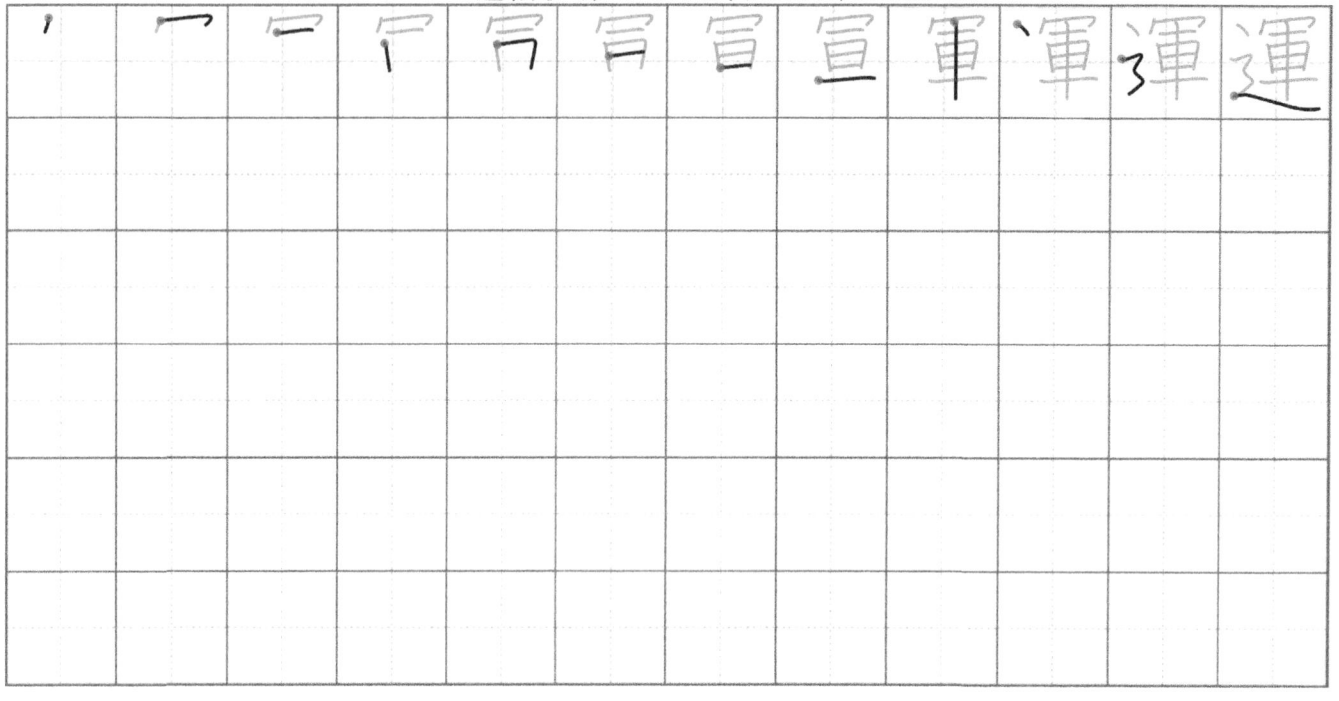

道

road-way; street; teachings

onyomi	トウ、ドウ
kunyomi	みち
compounds	柔道 (じゅうどう) judo
	水道 (すいどう) water supply; water works
	道 (みち) road; street
	道具 (どうぐ) tool; apparatus; device

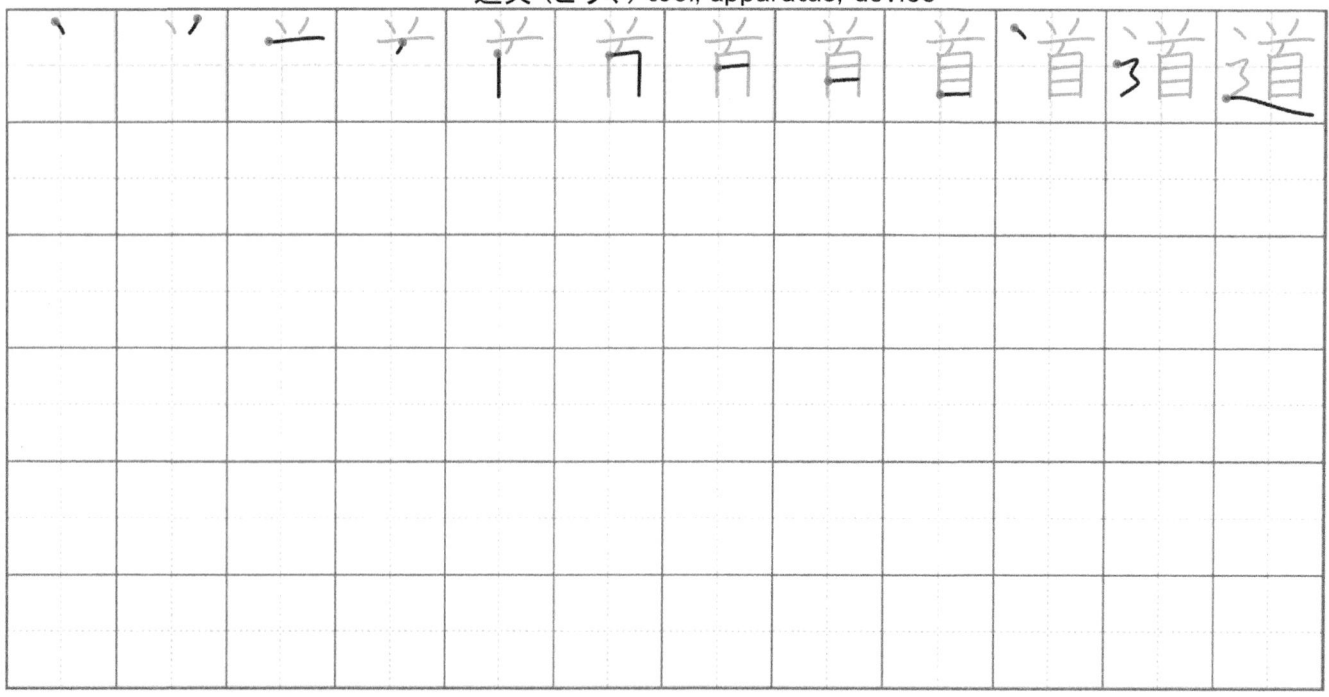

遠

far

onyomi エン、オン
kunyomi とお・い
compounds 遠い（とおい）far; distant
遠く（とおく）far away; distant
遠慮（えんりょ）holding back (out of politeness)

一	十	土	圭	吉	吉	声	表	袁	袁	袁	遠
遠											

都

capital; metropolis

onyomi ツ、ト
kunyomi みやこ
compounds 都（と）metropolis; city
都合（つごう）circumstances; condition | arrangement

一	十	土	才	者	者	者	者	者	都	都	

重

onyomi　ジュウ、チョウ
kunyomi　おも・い、かさ・なる、かさ・ねる
compounds　重い（おもい）heavy; weighty

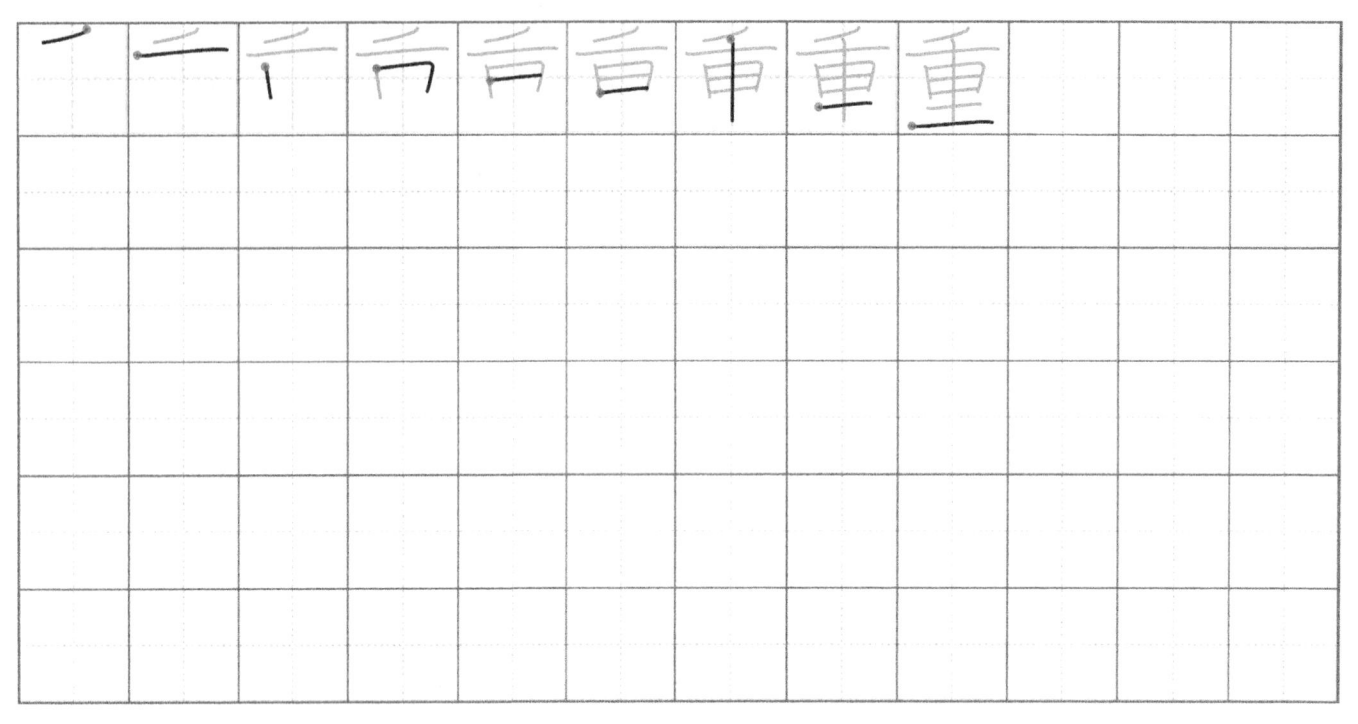

野

field; rustic

onyomi　ヤ
kunyomi　の
compounds　野菜（やさい）vegetable

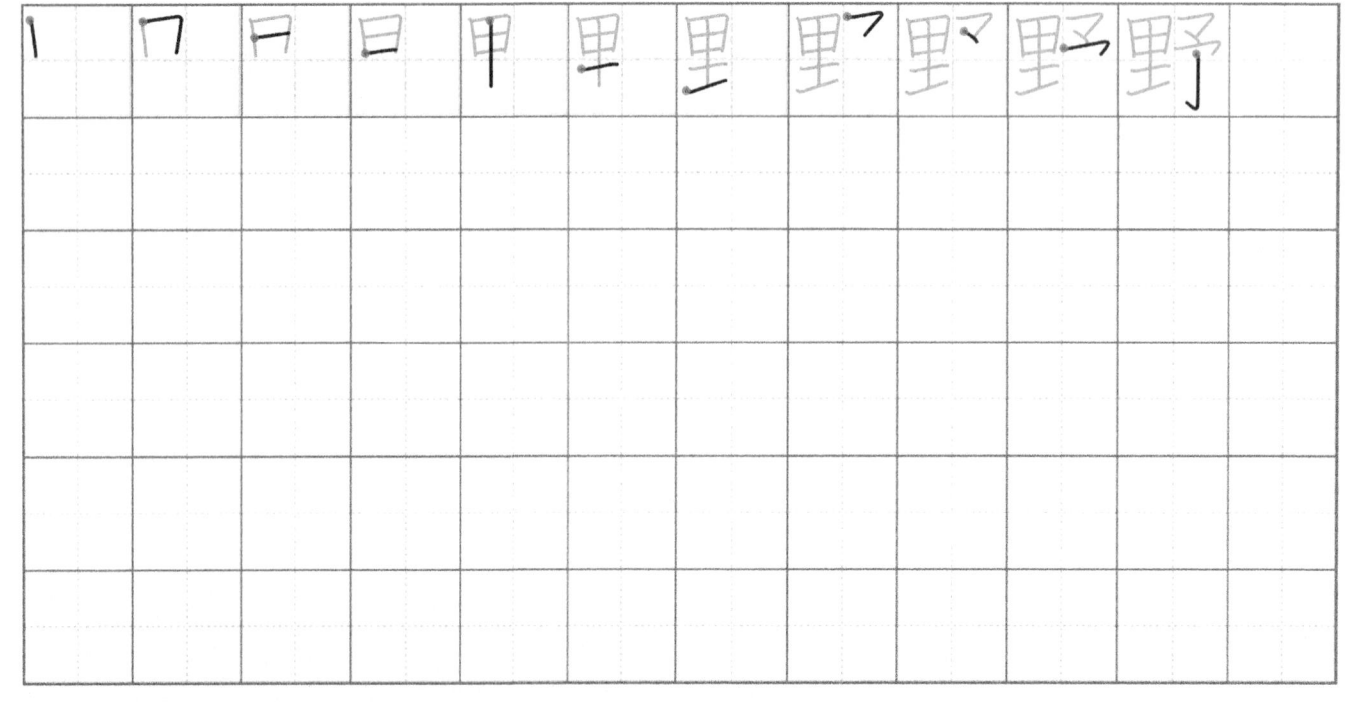

銀

onyomi　ギン
kunyomi　しろがね
compounds　銀行 (ぎんこう) bank

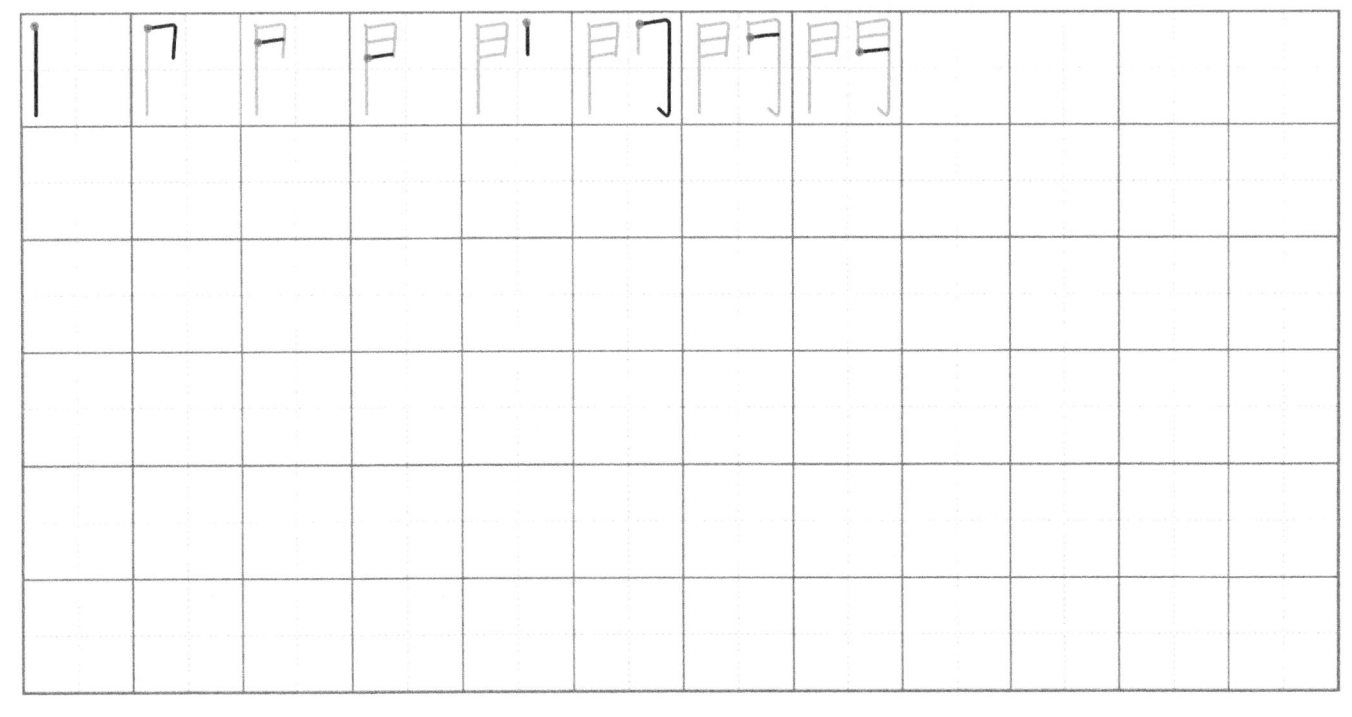

門

gate

onyomi　モン
kunyomi　かど
compounds　専門 (せんもん) speciality; area of expertise
　　　　　　門 (もん) gate

開

open; unfold

onyomi	カイ
kunyomi	あ・く、あ・ける、ひら・く、ひら・ける
compounds	開く（あく）to open (e.g. doors)
	開く（ひらく）（ひらく）to open
	開ける（あける）to open (a door, etc.); to unwrap; to unlock

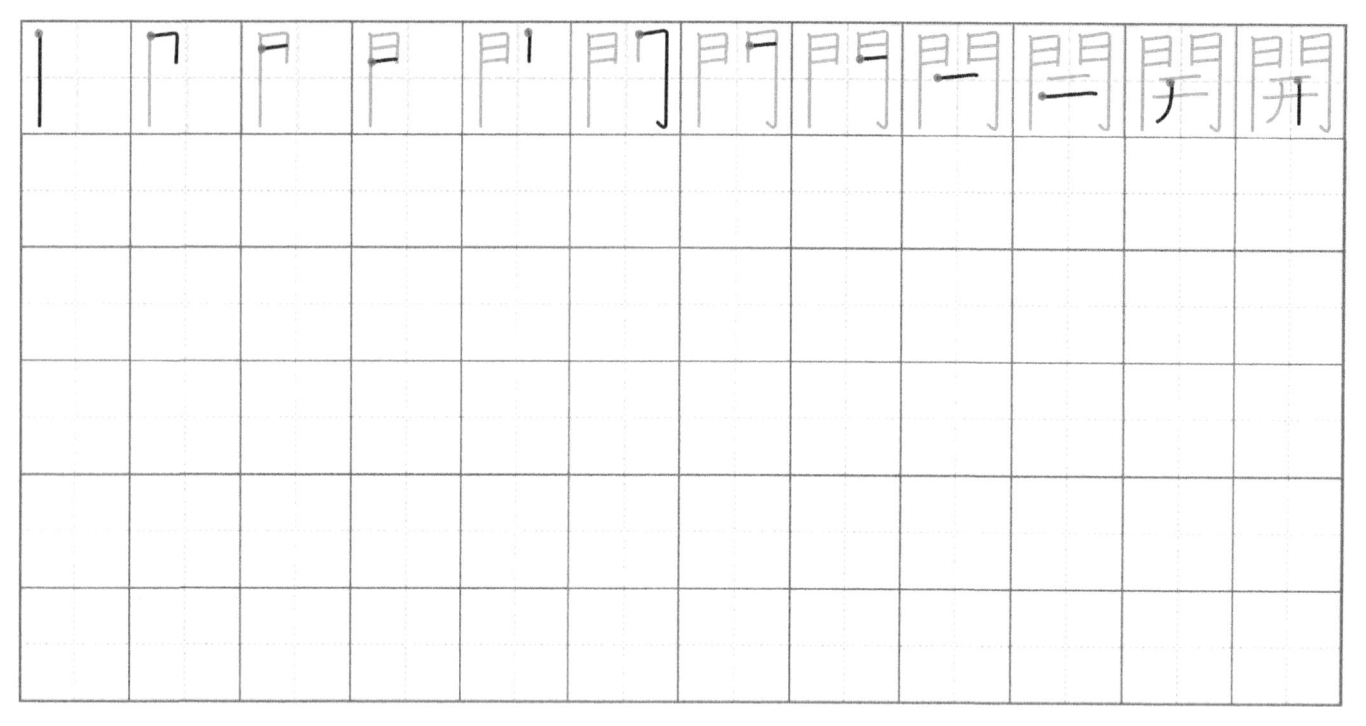

院

institution

onyomi	イン
kunyomi	
compounds	入院（にゅういん）hospitalization
	病院（びょういん）hospital
	退院（たいいん）discharge from hospital

flock; gather

onyomi	シュウ
kunyomi	あつ・まる、あつ・める
compounds	集まる（あつまる）to gather
	集める（あつめる）to collect; to assemble; to gather

blue; green

onyomi	ショウ、セイ
kunyomi	あお、あお・い
compounds	青（あお）blue; green
	青い（あおい）blue; green

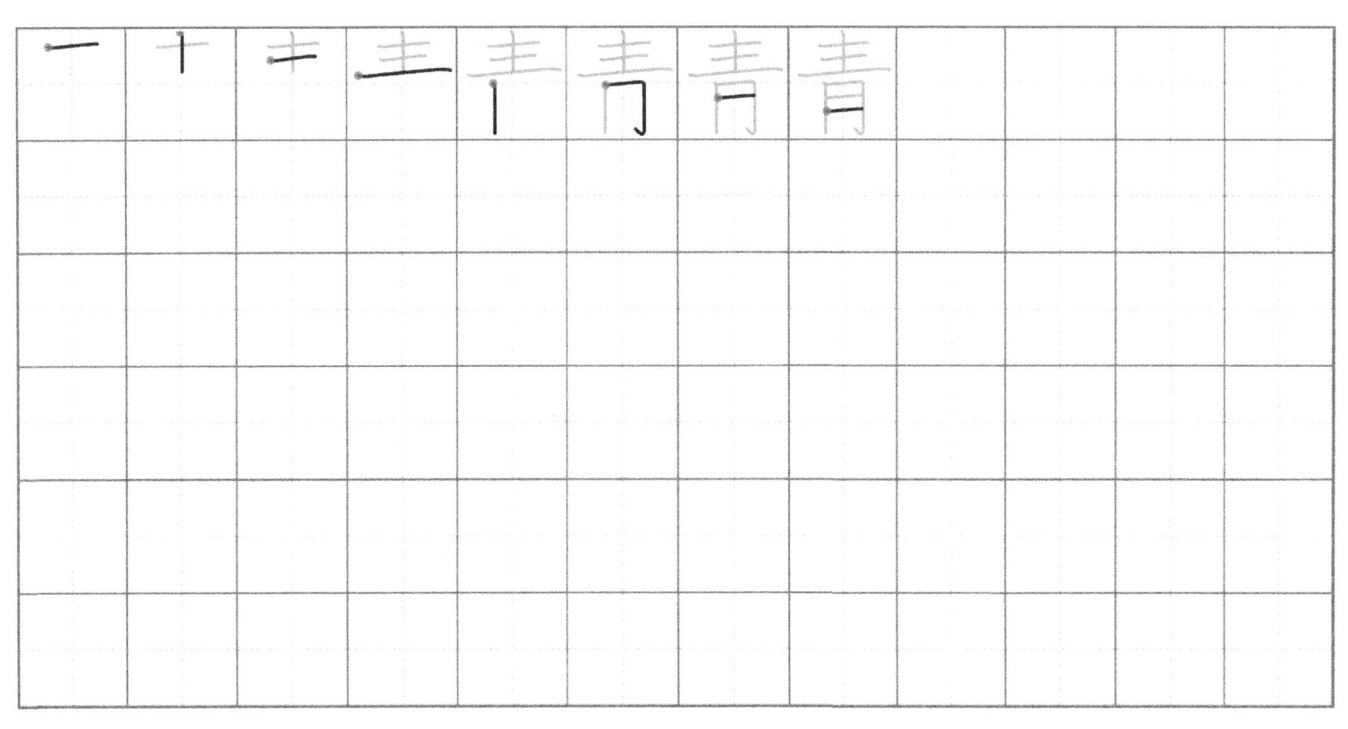

音

noise; sound

onyomi	イン、オン
kunyomi	おと、ね
compounds	発音 (はつおん) pronunciation
	音 (おと) sound; noise
	音楽 (おんがく) music

頭

head

onyomi	ズ、ト、トウ
kunyomi	あたま、かしら
compounds	頭 (あたま) head

音、頭

subject; topic

onyomi	ダイ
kunyomi	
compounds	問題（もんだい）question (e.g. on a test); problem
	宿題（しゅくだい）homework; assignment

expression; face

onyomi	ガン
kunyomi	かお
compounds	顔（かお）face | look; expression

air; manner; style; wind

onyomi	フ、フウ
kunyomi	かぜ
compounds	台風 (たいふう) typhoon; hurricane
	風 (かぜ) wind; breeze
	風呂 (ふろ) bath; bathhouse
	風邪 (かぜ) common cold

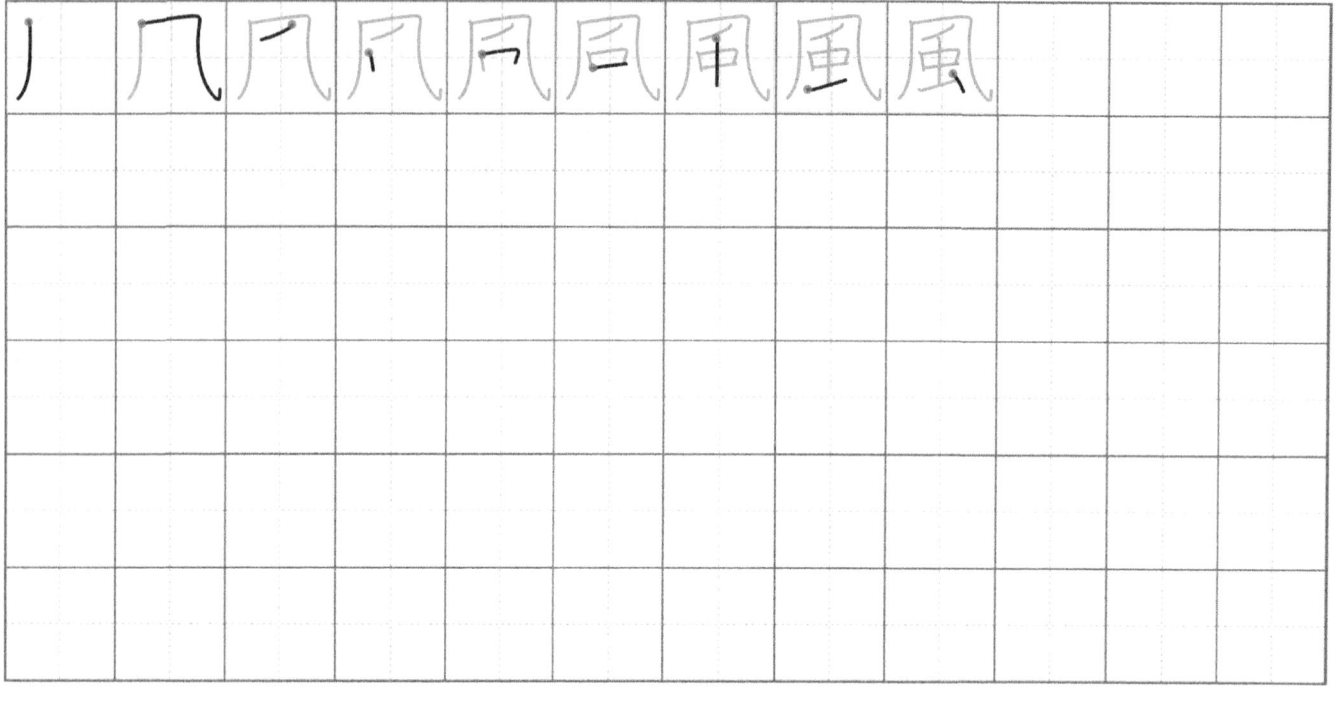

boiled rice; meal

onyomi	ハン
kunyomi	めし
compounds	夕飯 (ゆうめし、ゆうはん) evening meal
	御飯 (ごはん) cooked rice | meal
	晩御飯 (ばんごはん) dinner

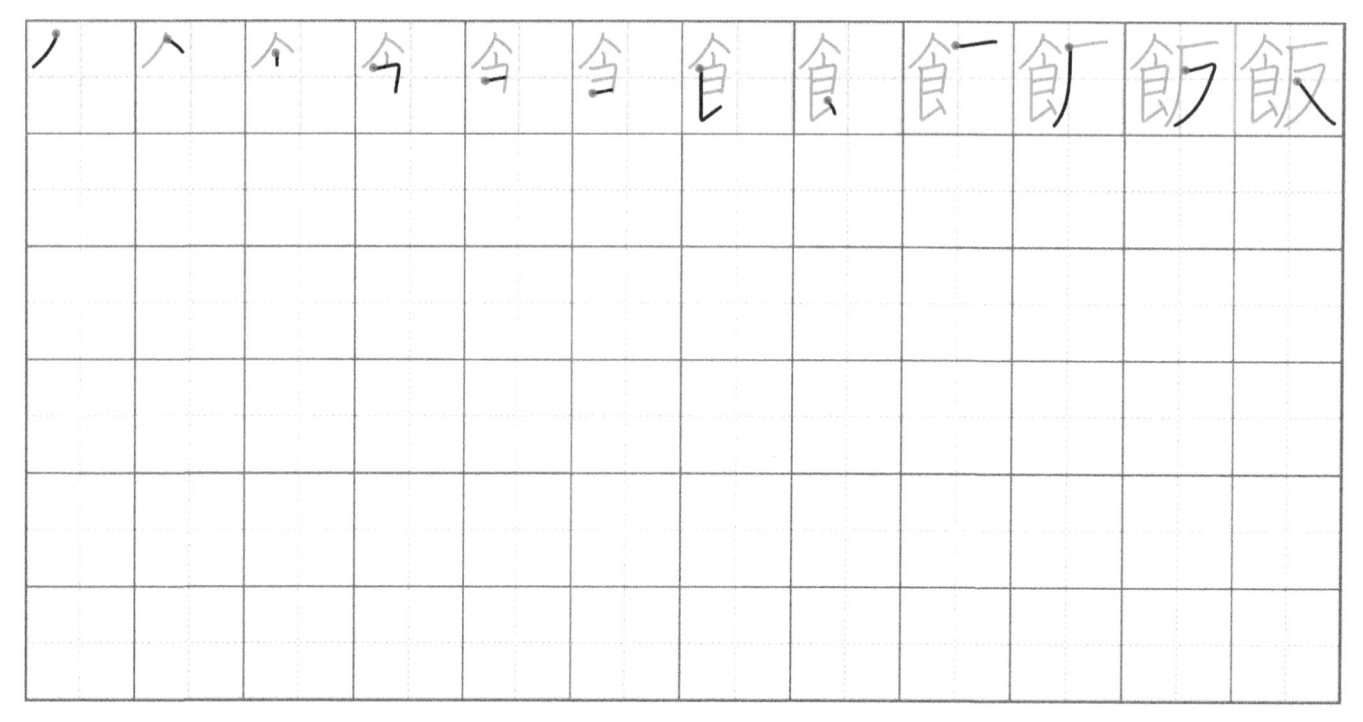

飲

<u>drink</u>

onyomi イン
kunyomi の・む
compounds 飲み物 (のみもの) drink; beverage
飲む (のむ) to drink; to swallow; to take (medicine)

館

<u>(large) building</u>

onyomi カン
kunyomi やかた
compounds 図書館 (としょかん) library
旅館 (りょかん) Japanese-style lodging
映画館 (えいがかん) movie theatre
美術館 (びじゅつかん) art museum

飲、館

99

首

neck

onyomi　シュ
kunyomi　くび
compounds　首（くび）neck

｀　　ツ　　ソ　　ヤ　　艹　　首　　首　　首　　首

駅

station

onyomi　エキ
kunyomi
compounds　駅（えき）station

丨　　厂　　冂　　𠃌　　馬　　馬　　馬　　馬　　馬　　馬　　駅　　駅

駅　駅

験

testing; verification

onyomi ケン、ゲン
kunyomi
compounds 経験 (けいけん) experience
試験 (しけん) exam; test

魚

fish

onyomi ギョ
kunyomi さかな
compounds 魚 (さかな) fish

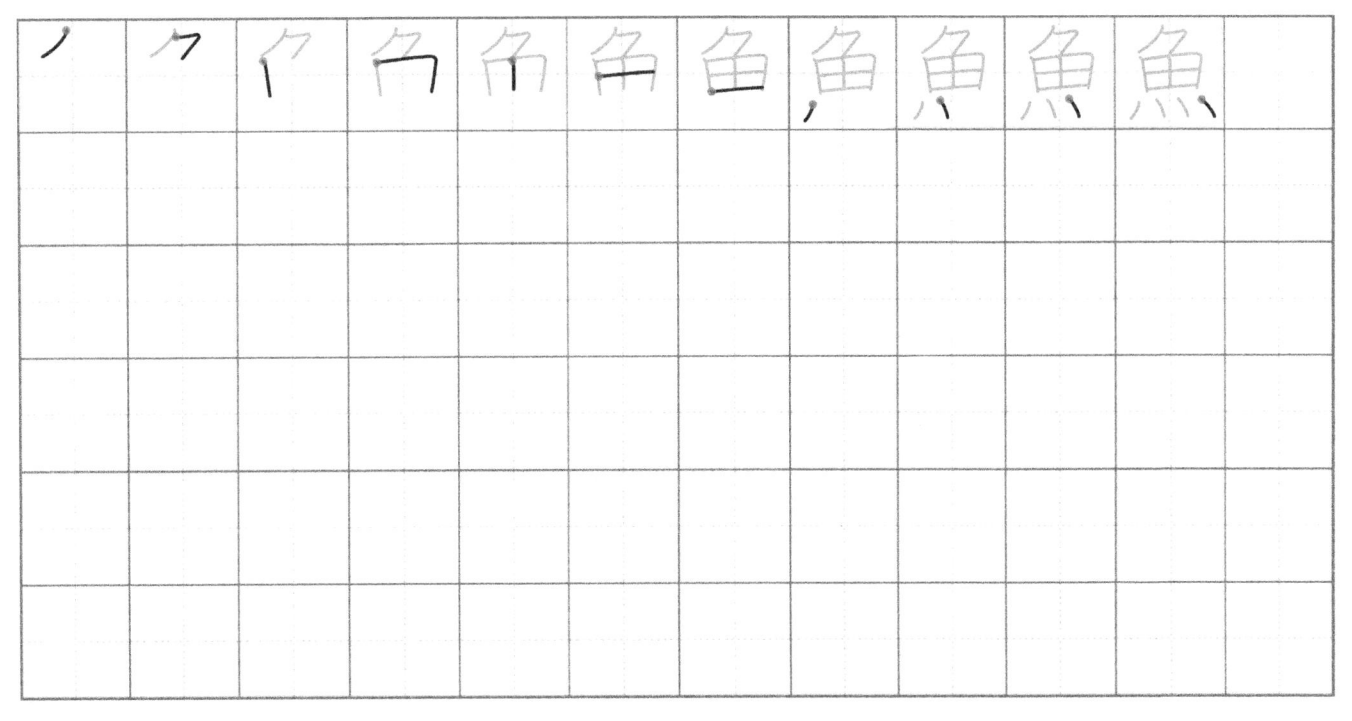

鳥

<u>bird; chicken</u>

onyomi	チョウ
kunyomi	とり
compounds	小鳥 (ことり) small bird
	鳥 (とり) bird

黒

<u>black</u>

onyomi	コク
kunyomi	くろ、くろ・い
compounds	黒 (くろ) black
	黒い (くろい) black

(〜しゅうかん) period of weeks

〜週間

(〜かいだて) 〜-storied building

〜階建て

(おみやげ) present; souvenir

お土産

(おてあらい) toilet; restroom

お手洗い

(ごしゅじん (hon) your husband)

ご主人

(いちど) once

一度

(じょうず) skillful; proficient; good (at)

上手

(うわぎ) coat; tunic; jacket; outer garment

上着

(したぎ) underwear

下着

(ふべん) inconvenience

不便

(せかい) world

世界

(せわ) looking after

世話

(りょうほう) both; both sides

両方

(りょうしん) both parents

両親

(のりかえる) to transfer/change (bus, train)

乗り換える

(のりもの) vehicle

乗り物

(よしゅう) preparation for a lesson

予習

(じむしょ) office

事務所

(じこ) accident; incident; trouble

事故

(こうつう) traffic; transportation; communication

交通

(きょうと) Kyoto

京都

(じんこう) population

人口

(こんや) this evening; tonight

今夜

(こんど) next time; another time

今度

(けさ) this morning

今朝

(こんしゅう) this week

今週

(しごと) work; job; business

仕事

(しかた) way; method; means

仕方

(いじょう) more than (or equal to); at least

以上

(いか) less than (or equal to); below

以下

(いない) within; up to; less than

以 内

(いがい) with the exception of; other than

以 外

(かいじょう) assembly hall; venue

会 場

(かいしゃ) company

会 社

(かいしゃいん) company employee

会 社 員

(かいぎしつ) conference room

会 議 室

(じゅうしょ) address (e.g. of house)

住 所

(さくぶん) writing; composition

作 文

(べんり) convenient; handy; useful

便 利

(げんき) healthy; well; lively

元 気

(きょうだい) siblings; brothers and sisters

兄弟

(いりぐち) entrance; entry

入口

(にゅういん) hospitalization

入院

(やおや) greengrocer

八百屋

(こうむいん) government worker

公務員

(こうえん) park

公園

(しゃしん) photograph; photo; picture

写真

(でぐち) exit

出口

(しゅっぱつ) departure

出発

(きって) stamp (postage)

切手

(きっぷ) ticket

切符

(りよう) use; utilization

利用

(べんきょう) study

勉強

(どうぶつ) animal

動物

(どうぶつえん) zoo

動物園

(いがく) medical science; medicine

医学

(いしゃ) doctor

医者

(ちばけん) Chiba Prefeture

千葉県

(そつぎょう) graduation

卒業

(きょねん) last year

去年

(だいどころ) kitchen

台所

(たいふう) typhoon; hurricane

台風

(みそ) (food) miso

味噌

(しなもの) goods; article

品物

(もんだい) question (e.g. on a test); problem

問題

(きっさてん) coffee shop; cafe

喫茶店

(としょかん) library

図書館

(どようび) Saturday

土曜日

(ちかてつ) subway

地下鉄

(ちず) map

地図

(ちり) geography

地理

(じしん) earthquake

地震

(ばあい) case; situation

場合

(ばしょ) place; location

場所

(うりば) place where things are sold (sales counter, corner, etc.)

売り場

(なつやすみ) summer vacation

夏休み

(ゆうがた) evening; dusk

夕方

(ゆうめし、ゆうはん) evening meal

夕飯

(たぶん) perhaps; probably

多分

(だいたい) generally; approximately

大体

(たいしかん) embassy

大使館

(たいせつ) important; necessary

大切

(だいすき) loveable; like very much

大好き

(じびき) dictionary

字引き

(あんぜん) safety; security

安全

(あんしん) relief; peace of mind

安心

(かない) (hum) wife | one's family

家内

(かてい) household; family

家庭

(かぞく) family; members of a family

家族

(しゅくだい) homework; assignment

宿題

(せんもん) speciality; area of expertise

専門

(しょうせつ) novel; (short) story

小説

(ことり) small bird

小鳥

(おくじょう) rooftop

屋上

(こうじょう、こうば) factory; plant; mill; workshop

工場

(こうぎょう) industry; industrial

工業

(しみん) city resident; townspeople

市民

(てんいん) clerk; salesperson

店員

(たてもの) building

建物

(ひきだし) drawer

引き出し

(ひきだす) to pull out; to bring out; to withdraw

引き出す

(ひっこす) to move; to change residence

引っ越す

(やくにたつ) to be useful

役に立つ

(ごはん) cooked rice | meal

御飯

(ふくしゅう) review

復習

(しんぱい) worry; concern

心配

(おもいだす) to recall; to remember

思い出す

(きゅうこう) express (train)

急行

(いみ) meaning

意味

(いけん) opinion

意見

(てつだう) to help; to assist

手伝う

(てがみ) letter

手紙

(しょうち) consent; acceptance

承知

(しょうたい) invitation

招待

(じゅぎょう) lesson; class work

授業

(したく) preparation; arrangements

支度

(ほうそう) broadcast

放送

(きょうかい) church

教会

(きょうしつ) classroom

教室

(きょういく) education; schooling; training

教育

(さんぽ) walk; stroll

散歩

(ぶんか) culture

文化

(ぶんがく) literature

文学

(ぶんぽう) grammar

文法

(ぶんしょう) writing; composition | sentence

文章

(りょうり) cooking; cuisine

料理

(しんぶん) newspaper

新聞

(しんぶんしゃ) newspaper company

新聞社

(りょこう) trip

旅行

(りょかん) Japanese-style lodging

旅館

(にちようび) Sunday

日 曜 日

(あした) tomorrow

明 日

(えいが) movie; film

映 画

(えいがかん) movie theatre

映 画 館

(ゆうべ) last night

昨 夜

(ひるやすみ) lunch (noon) break

昼 休 み

(ひるごはん) lunch

昼 御 飯

(ひるま) daytime; during the day

昼 間

(じだい) period; era; times

時 代

(とけい) watch; clock

時 計

Compound words practice

(ばんごはん) dinner

晩御飯

(ふつう) usual; ordinary

普通

(けしき) scenery; scene; landscape

景色

(さいきん) recently

最近

(げつようび) Monday

月曜日

(ゆうめい) famous

有名

(あさごはん) breakfast

朝御飯

(らいしゅう) next week

来週

(くだもの) fruit

果物

(じゅうどう) judo

柔道

(しょうがつ) New Year (esp. the first few days); January

正月

(はいしゃ) dentist

歯医者

(まいあさ) every morning

毎朝

(まいしゅう) every week

毎週

(きもち) feeling; sensation; mood

気持ち

(すいどう) water supply; water works

水道

(ちゅうしゃ) injection; shot

注射

(ちゅうい) caution; attention; warning

注意

(ようふく) Western-style clothes

洋服

(せんたく) washing; laundry

洗濯

(かいがん) coast; beach

海岸

(しぶやく) Shibuya

渋谷区

(かんじ) Chinese characters; kanji

漢字

(まんが) cartoon; comic

漫画

(むり) impossible

無理

(ねっしん) zeal; enthusiasm

熱心

(ぎゅうにゅう) (cow's) milk

牛乳

(ぎゅうにく) beef

牛肉

(とくべつ) special

特別

(とっきゅう) limited express (train, faster than an express)

特急

(りゆう) reason; motive

理由

(せいさん) production; manufacture

生産

(さんぎょう) industry

産業

(ようじ) things to do; errand; business (to take care of)

用事

(ようい) preparation; arrangements

用意

(いなか) rural area; countryside

田舎

(びょうき) illness; disease

病気

(びょういん) hospital

病院

(はつおん) pronunciation

発音

(まんなか) middle; center

真中

(まじめ) diligent; serious; honest

真面目

(きもの) kimono (or other trad. Japanese clothing)

着物

(けんきゅう) study; research

研究

(けんきゅうしつ) laboratory

研究室

(しゃかい) society

社会

(しゃちょう) company president

社長

(じんじゃ) Shinto shrine

神社

(くうき) air; atmosphere | mood; situation

空気

(くうこう) airport

空港

(りっぱ) splendid; fine

立派

(こうちゃ) black tea

紅茶

(けいけん) experience

経験

(れんしゅう) practice

練習

(びじゅつかん) art museum

美術館

(しゅうかん) habit; custom

習慣

(じぶん) myself; oneself

自分

(じどうしゃ) automobile

自動車

(じゆう) freedom

自由

(じてんしゃ) bicycle

自転車

(きょうみ) interest (in something); curiosity

興味

(いろいろ) various

色々

(かびん) (flower) vase

花瓶

(はなみ) cherry blossom viewing

花見

(えいご) English

英語

(ちゃいろ) brown

茶色

(にもつ) luggage; package

荷物

(せいよう) the west; Western countries

西洋

(けんぶつ) sightseeing; watching

見物

(しんせつ) kindness; gentleness

親切

(ことば) word; phrase

言葉

(けいかく) plan; schedule

計画

(しあい) match; game

試合

(しけん) exam; test

試験

(せつめい) explanation; exposition

説明

(こうどう) auditorium; lecture hall

講堂

(ぶたにく) pork

豚肉

(かいもの) shopping; purchased goods

買い物

(しつもん) question; inquiry

質問

(あかんぼう) baby; infant

赤ん坊

(しゅみ) hobby

趣味

(きんじょ) neighborhood

近所

(へんじ) reply; response

返事

(たいいん) discharge from hospital

退院

(うんどう) exercise; physical training

運動

(うんてん) operation (of a machine, etc.); driving

運転

(うんてんしゅ) driver; chauffeur

運転手

(どうぐ) tool; apparatus; device

道具

(えんりょ) holding back (out of politeness)

遠慮

(へや) room

部屋

(ゆうびんきょく) post office

郵便局

(つごう) circumstances; condition | arrangement

都合

(やさい) vegetable

野菜

(かねもち) rich person

金持ち

(ぎんこう) bank

銀行

(まにあう) to be in time for

間に合う

(おんがく) music

音楽

(ふろ) bath; bathhouse

風呂

(かぜ) common cold

風邪

(しょくどう) cafeteria

食堂

(しょくりょうひん) foodstuff; groceries

食料品

(のみもの) drink; beverage

飲み物

(ちゅうしゃじょう) parking lot

駐車場

(とりにく) chicken meat

鶏肉

(きいろい) yellow

黄色い

(くつした) socks

靴下

(がいこくじん) foreigner; foreign citizen

外国人

(せんせい) teacher; doctor

先生

(せんしゅう) last week

先週

(はんぶん) half

半分

(なまえ) name | given name; first name

名前

(ごぜん) morning; a.m.

午前

(ともだち) friend; companion

友達

(ひらがな) hiragana

平仮名

(だいがく) university; college

大学

(てんき) weather

天気

(ぼうし) hat

帽子

(こども) child; children

子供

(がっこう) school

学校

(ことし) this year

今年

(はがき) postcard

葉書

Compound words practice

128

世 不

乗 主

京 事

代 仕

会 以

generation; public; society; world

onyomi
セ、セイ、ソウ

kunyomi
よ

non-; negative; bad

onyomi
フ、ブ

kunyomi

board; ride; counter for vehicles; multiplication; power

onyomi
ショウ、ジョウ

kunyomi
の・せる、の・る

chief; lord; main thing; master; principal

onyomi
シュ、シュウ、ス

kunyomi
おも、ぬし

capital

onyomi
キョウ

kunyomi
みやこ

business; fact; matter; possibly; reason; thing

onyomi
ジ

kunyomi
こと

change; replace; substitute; convert; counter for decades of ages; fee; generation; period

onyomi
タイ、ダイ

kunyomi
かわ・る、か・える

attend; doing; official; serve

onyomi
シ、ジ

kunyomi
つか・える

association; interview; join; meet; meeting; party

onyomi
エ、カイ

kunyomi
あ・う、あ・わせる、あつ・まる

because; by means of; compared with

onyomi
イ

kunyomi

住	低
作	体
便	使
働	借
兄	元

live; reside

onyomi

ジュウ、チュウ、ヂュウ

kunyomi

す・まう、す・む

build; make; prepare; production

onyomi

サ、サク

kunyomi

つく・り、つく・る

convenience; facility; feces; letter

onyomi

ビン、ベン

kunyomi

たよ・り

work

onyomi

ドウ

kunyomi

はたら・く

elder brother

onyomi

キョウ

kunyomi

あに

humble; lower; short

onyomi

テイ

kunyomi

ひく・い、ひく・まる、ひく・める

body; object; substance

onyomi

タイ、テイ

kunyomi

かたち、からだ

ambassador; use

onyomi

シ

kunyomi

つか・い、つか・う

borrow; rent

onyomi

シャク

kunyomi

か・りる

beginning; origin; former time

onyomi

ガン、ゲン

kunyomi

もと

光	公
写	冬
切	別
力	勉
動	区

governmental; public

onyomi
ク、コウ

kunyomi
おおやけ

light; ray

onyomi
コウ

kunyomi
ひか・る

winter

onyomi
トウ

kunyomi
ふゆ

copy

onyomi
シャ、ジャ

kunyomi
うつ・す、うつ・る

branch off; fork; separate

onyomi
ベツ

kunyomi
わか・れる、わ・ける

be sharp; cut

onyomi
サイ、セツ

kunyomi
き・る、き・れる

diligent; make effort; strive

onyomi
ベン

kunyomi
つと・める

power; strength

onyomi
リイ、リキ、リョク

kunyomi
ちから

district; ward

onyomi
ク、コウ

kunyomi

change; confusion; motion; move; shake; shift

onyomi
ドウ

kunyomi
うご・かす、うご・く

去　医

古　口

合　台

味　同

員　品

eliminate; leave; past; quit onyomi キョ、コ kunyomi さ・る	**doctor; medicine** onyomi イ kunyomi い・する、い・やす
old onyomi コ kunyomi ふる・い	**mouth** onyomi ク、コウ kunyomi くち
fit; join onyomi カッ、ガッ、ゴウ kunyomi あ・う、あ・わせる	**a stand; counter for machines and vehicles** onyomi タイ、ダイ kunyomi つかさ
flavor; taste onyomi ミ kunyomi あじ、あじ・わう	**agree; equal; same** onyomi ドウ kunyomi おな・じ
employee; member onyomi イン kunyomi	**goods; refinement** onyomi ヒン kunyomi しな

回	問
地	図
場	堂
売	声
夕	夏

～ times; revolve

onyomi
カイ

kunyomi
まわ・す、まわ・る

earth; ground

onyomi
ジ、チ

kunyomi

location; place

onyomi
ジョウ

kunyomi
ば

sell

onyomi
バイ

kunyomi
う・る、う・れる

evening

onyomi

kunyomi
ゆう

ask; problem; question

onyomi
モン

kunyomi
と・う

map; plan

onyomi
ズ、ト

kunyomi
はか・る

hall

onyomi
ドウ

kunyomi

voice

onyomi
ショウ、セイ

kunyomi
こえ

summer

onyomi
カ、ガ

kunyomi
なつ

多	夜
太	好
妹	姉
始	字
安	室

evening

onyomi
ヤ

kunyomi
よ、よる

frequent; many

onyomi
タ

kunyomi
おお・い

fond; pleasing

onyomi
コウ

kunyomi
この・む、す・く

plump; thick

onyomi
タ、タイ

kunyomi
ふと・い、ふと・る

elder sister

onyomi
シ

kunyomi
あね

younger sister

onyomi
マイ

kunyomi
いもうと

character; letter

onyomi
ジ

kunyomi
あざ

begin

onyomi
シ

kunyomi
はじ・まる、はじ・める

chamber; room

onyomi
シツ

kunyomi

cheap; peaceful; relaxed

onyomi
アン

kunyomi
やす・い、やす・まる

寒	家
屋	少
市	工
広	帰
度	店

cold

onyomi

カン

kunyomi

さむ・い

family; home; expert; professional

onyomi

カ、ケ

kunyomi

いえ、うち、や

house; roof; shop

onyomi

オク

kunyomi

や

few

onyomi

ショウ

kunyomi

すく・ない、すこ・し

city; market

onyomi

シ

kunyomi

いち

construction; craft; katakana e radical (no. 48)

onyomi

ク、コウ

kunyomi

wide

onyomi

コウ

kunyomi

ひろ・い、ひろ・がる、ひろ・げる、ひろ・まる、ひろ・める

come home

onyomi

キ

kunyomi

かえ・る

degrees; occurrence; time

onyomi

タク、ド

kunyomi

たび

shop; store

onyomi

テン

kunyomi

みせ

引	建
弱	弟
待	強
思	心
悪	急

pull

onyomi
イン

kunyomi
ひ・く、ひ・ける

frail; weak

onyomi
ジャク

kunyomi
よわ・い、よわ・まる、よわ・める

depend on; wait

onyomi
タイ

kunyomi
ま・つ

think

onyomi
シ

kunyomi
おも・う

bad; evil

onyomi
アク

kunyomi
わる・い

build

onyomi
ケン

kunyomi
た・つ、た・てる

younger brother

onyomi
ダイ

kunyomi
おとうと

strong

onyomi
キョウ、ゴウ

kunyomi
つよ・い、つよ・まる、つよ・める

heart; mind; spirit

onyomi
シン

kunyomi
こころ

emergency; hurry

onyomi
キュウ

kunyomi
いそ・ぎ、いそ・ぐ

所	意
持	手
文	教
新	料
旅	方

extent; place

onyomi
ショ
kunyomi
ところ、どころ

care; desire; thought

onyomi
イ
kunyomi

have; hold

onyomi
ジ
kunyomi
も・つ、も・てる

hand

onyomi
シュ、ズ
kunyomi
て

art; decoration; literature

onyomi
ブン、モン
kunyomi
あや、ふみ

doctrine; faith; teach

onyomi
キョウ
kunyomi
おし・える、おそ・わる

new

onyomi
シン
kunyomi
あたら・しい、あら・た

fee; materials

onyomi
リョウ
kunyomi

travel; trip

onyomi
リョ
kunyomi
たび

alternative; person

onyomi
ホウ
kunyomi
かた

早	族
映	明
昼	春
暗	暑
有	曜

early; fast

onyomi
サッ、ソウ
kunyomi
はや・い、はや・まる、はや・める

projection; reflection

onyomi
エイ
kunyomi
うつ・す、うつ・る、は・える

daytime; noon

onyomi
チュウ
kunyomi
ひる

darkness; grow dark

onyomi
アン
kunyomi
くら・い、くら・む、くれ・る

exist; happen; possess

onyomi
ユウ
kunyomi
あ・る

family; tribe

onyomi
ゾク
kunyomi

bright; light

onyomi
ミョウ、メイ
kunyomi
あか・るい、あき・らか、あ・かり

springtime

onyomi
シュン
kunyomi
はる

hot; sultry

onyomi
ショ
kunyomi
あつ・い

weekday

onyomi
ヨウ
kunyomi

服	朝
村	林
森	業
楽	歌
止	正

morning; dynasty; period

onyomi

チョウ

kunyomi

あさ

clothing

onyomi

フク

kunyomi

forest; grove

onyomi

リン

kunyomi

はやし

town; village

onyomi

ソン

kunyomi

むら

arts; vocation

onyomi

ギョウ、ゴウ

kunyomi

わざ

forest; woods

onyomi

シン

kunyomi

もり

sing; song

onyomi

カ

kunyomi

うた、うた・う

comfort; ease

onyomi

ガク、ゴウ、ラク

kunyomi

この・む、たの・しい、たの・しむ

correct

onyomi

ショウ、セイ

kunyomi

ただ・しい、まさ・に

halt; stop

onyomi

シ

kunyomi

とど・まる、とど・める、と・まる、と・める、や・む、や・める

死 歩

池 民

洋 注

海 洗

牛 漢

death

onyomi
シ

kunyomi
し・ぬ

---

pond; pool

onyomi
チ

kunyomi
いけ

---

ocean; sea; Western style; foreign

onyomi
ヨウ

kunyomi

---

ocean

onyomi
カイ

kunyomi
うみ

---

cow

onyomi
ギュウ

kunyomi
うし

---

counter for steps; walk

onyomi
フ、ブ、ホ

kunyomi
あゆ・む、ある・く

---

nation; people

onyomi
ミン

kunyomi
たみ

---

annotate; comment; concentrate on; flow into

onyomi
チュウ

kunyomi
さ・す、そそ・ぐ、つ・ぐ

---

inquire into; probe; wash

onyomi
セン

kunyomi
あら・う

China; Sino-

onyomi
カン

kunyomi

物　特

犬　理

産　用

田　町

画　界

special

onyomi

トク

kunyomi

---

matter; object; thing

onyomi

ブツ、モツ

kunyomi

もの

---

arrangement; justice; logic; reason

onyomi

リ

kunyomi

ことわり

---

dog

onyomi

ケン

kunyomi

いぬ

---

business; employ; use

onyomi

ヨウ

kunyomi

もち・いる

---

childbirth; native; products; property

onyomi

サン

kunyomi

う・まれる、う・む

---

block; street; town; village

onyomi

チョウ

kunyomi

まち

---

rice field; rice paddy

onyomi

デン

kunyomi

た

---

boundary; world

onyomi

カイ

kunyomi

---

brush-stroke; picture

onyomi

エ、カク、ガ

kunyomi

えが・く、はか・る

発	病
県	目
着	真
短	知
社	研

departure; disclose; emit; publish; start from

onyomi

ハツ、ホツ

kunyomi

た・つ、つか・わす、はな・つ

prefecture

onyomi

ケン

kunyomi

arrive; don; wear

onyomi

ジャク、チャク

kunyomi

き・せる、き・る、つ・く、つ・ける

brevity; short; defect; fault

onyomi

タン

kunyomi

みじか・い

association; company; shrine

onyomi

シャ

kunyomi

やしろ

ill; sick

onyomi

ビョウ

kunyomi

やまい、や・む

eye; insight; experience; favor

onyomi

ボク、モク

kunyomi

め

Buddhist sect; reality; true

onyomi

シン

kunyomi

ま、まこと

know; wisdom

onyomi

チ

kunyomi

し・らせる、し・る

polish; sharpen

onyomi

ケン

kunyomi

と・ぐ

私	秋
究	空
立	答
紙	終
習	考

autumn

onyomi
シュウ
kunyomi
あき

I; me; private

onyomi
シ
kunyomi
わたくし、わたし

empty; vacuum; sky

onyomi
クウ
kunyomi
あ・く、あ・ける、から、す・く

research; study

onyomi
キュウ、ク
kunyomi
きわ・める

answer; solution

onyomi
トウ
kunyomi
こた・える

erect; rise; stand up

onyomi
リツ、リュウ
kunyomi
た・つ、た・てる

end; finish

onyomi
シュウ
kunyomi
お・える、お・わる

paper

onyomi
シ
kunyomi
かみ

consider

onyomi
コウ
kunyomi
かんが・える

learn

onyomi
シュウ
kunyomi
なら・う

肉	者
色	自
英	花
菜	茶
親	薬

meat

onyomi
ニク

kunyomi

color

onyomi
シキ、ショク

kunyomi
いろ

England; English

onyomi
エイ

kunyomi

greens; vegetable

onyomi
サイ

kunyomi
な

parent; relative; intimacy

onyomi
シン

kunyomi
おや、した・しい、した・しむ

person

onyomi
シャ

kunyomi
もの

oneself

onyomi
シ、ジ

kunyomi
みずか・ら

flower

onyomi
カ

kunyomi
はな

tea

onyomi
サ、チャ

kunyomi

chemical; medicine

onyomi
ヤク

kunyomi
くすり

言

試

買

質

走

計

説

貸

赤

起

measure; plan

onyomi
ケイ

kunyomi
はか・る

explanation; opinion

onyomi
セツ、ゼイ

kunyomi
と・く

lend

onyomi
タイ

kunyomi
か・す

red

onyomi
シャク、セキ

kunyomi
あか、あか・い、あか・らむ、あか・らめ
る

get up; wake up

onyomi
キ

kunyomi
お・きる、お・こす、お・こる

say; word

onyomi
ゲン、ゴン

kunyomi
い・う

test; try

onyomi
シ

kunyomi
こころ・みる、ため・す

buy

onyomi
バイ

kunyomi
か・う

matter; quality

onyomi
シチ、シツ、チ

kunyomi

run

onyomi
ソウ

kunyomi
はし・る

転	足
近	軽
通	送
進	週
道	運

revolve

onyomi
テン
kunyomi
ころ・がす、ころ・がる、ころ・げる、ころ・ぶ

akin; near

onyomi
キン、コン
kunyomi
ちか・い

avenue; commute; pass through

onyomi
ツ、ツウ
kunyomi
かよ・う、とお・す、とお・る

advance; proceed

onyomi
シン
kunyomi
すす・む、すす・める

road-way; street; teachings

onyomi
トウ、ドウ
kunyomi
みち

leg; foot; be sufficient

onyomi
ソク
kunyomi
あし、た・す、た・りる、た・る

light; unimportant

onyomi
ケイ
kunyomi
かる・い、かろ・やか

escort; send

onyomi
ソウ
kunyomi
おく・る

week

onyomi
シュウ
kunyomi

carry; destiny; fate

onyomi
ウン
kunyomi
はこ・ぶ

遠	都
重	野
銀	門
開	院
集	青

capital; metropolis

onyomi
ツ、ト
kunyomi
みやこ

field; rustic

onyomi
ヤ
kunyomi
の

gate

onyomi
モン
kunyomi
かど

institution

onyomi
イン
kunyomi

blue; green

onyomi
ショウ、セイ
kunyomi
あお、あお・い

far

onyomi
エン、オン
kunyomi
とお・い

heavy; important; pile up

onyomi
ジュウ、チョウ
kunyomi
おも・い、かさ・なる、かさ・ねる

silver

onyomi
ギン
kunyomi
しろがね

open; unfold

onyomi
カイ
kunyomi
あ・く、あ・ける、ひら・く、ひら・ける

flock; gather

onyomi
シュウ
kunyomi
あつ・まる、あつ・める

音	頭
題	顔
風	飯
飲	館
首	駅

head

onyomi
ズ、ト、トウ
kunyomi
あたま、かしら

expression; face

onyomi
ガン
kunyomi
かお

boiled rice; meal

onyomi
ハン
kunyomi
めし

(large) building

onyomi
カン
kunyomi
やかた

station

onyomi
エキ
kunyomi

noise; sound

onyomi
イン、オン
kunyomi
おと、ね

subject; topic

onyomi
ダイ
kunyomi

air; manner; style; wind

onyomi
フ、フウ
kunyomi
かぜ

drink

onyomi
イン
kunyomi
の・む

neck

onyomi
シュ
kunyomi
くび

験

鳥

魚

黒

fish

onyomi
ギョ

kunyomi
さかな

black

onyomi
コク

kunyomi
くろ、くろ・い

testing; verification

onyomi
ケン、ゲン

kunyomi

bird; chicken

onyomi
チョウ

kunyomi
とり

Printed in Great Britain
by Amazon